I want to
borrow this !

Love Moe

Writing and Being

The Charles Eliot Norton Lectures, 1994

WRITING

AND

BEING

Nadine Gordimer

HARVARD UNIVERSITY PRESS
Cambridge, Massachusetts
London, England
1995

Library of Congress Cataloging-in-Publication Data

Gordimer, Nadine.
Writing and being / Nadine Gordimer.
p. cm. — (The Charles Eliot Norton lectures ; 1994)
Includes index.
ISBN 0-674-96232-X
1. Authors—20th century—Biography.   2. Gordimer, Nadine.   3. Literature and
revolutions.   4. Literature, Modern—Political aspects.   I. Title.   II. Series.
PN771.G67 1995
809′.04—dc20
[B]   95-17598
CIP

For Elena Levin

and to the memory of Professor Harry Levin

my dear friends and mentors

CONTENTS

WRITING AND BEING

1

ADAM'S RIB: FICTIONS AND REALITIES

What writer of fiction has not been affronted, when faced with journalists asking on which living personage this or that character is based? What writer has not read, in a review of her or his book, that so-and-so is clearly a portrait of such and such, and what writer has not been subjected to the curiosity of friends, acquaintances and even total strangers who would like to have their prurient guessing-game confirmed, a bull's eye scored on the writer as target?

By inference the very designation, 'writer of fiction', is perceived as itself fictitious. Literature is a tatty disguise to be gleefully unmasked; an intellectual cannibalism to be exposed. The writer's imagination is the looter among other people's lives.

Even writers themselves sometimes play the game with the work of other writers. And, of course, schools of criticism have flourished and fattened on it, in their day. Among non-professionals (critics are professionals; writers, like readers, are not; pen or word-processor has no tenure) it is not necessary for the player to know personally, have even the slightest acquaintance with, the supposed personage the writer has looted.

Looking back at my own youth, the radiant reading days of adolescence, I am puzzled to remember how, deep in D. H. Lawrence, I went through the local library in fervent pursuit of his circle as real-life counterparts of his characters. I pored over every publication of the Lawrence industry—from Freda's *Not I but the Wind* through Middleton Murry to those to whose canon Lawrence didn't belong but who 'took him up' between two fingers, the Bloomsbury group.

Of what possible significance could it have been to me, a sixteen-year-old autodidact living in a small gold-mining town in South Africa, to be told that the mother and Miriam, in *Sons and Lovers,* were Lawrence's own mother and his first love?

What could it matter to me that a rich bohemian eccentric, bizarrely named Ottoline, was rewarded for the house-party hospitality she granted the coal miner's genius son by appearing unflatteringly in one of his later novels?

What could be added to my understanding of, let alone pleasure in, the Lawrence novels and stories by my becoming privy to the gossip of men and women a world away, not only in distance but also in time, since I was eavesdropping during the Second World War, when the real personages who were purported to be the fictional ones I was familiar with were silenced by death or old age?

Perhaps the restricted context of my own burgeoning, the small variety of people I knew, and the boredom of lives treading the inevitable round of births, marriages, pregnancies, deaths, births, made me yearn to connect thrilling fictions as a

2

❦

realizable possibility with people who actually were alive once, as I now was, outside the transports of reading which ended with the turning of the last page.

Another explanation to myself is that, beginning to write before I had really lived (the great source of childhood is ready to be tapped, like a rubber tree, only after a certain stage of growth is reached), I was fumbling to find out where fiction came from, and how. I was looking for *the* methodology, presupposing a general one distinct from the imaginings going on, distrusted, in my own head.

Last year I was sent the gift of a 418-page biography of none other than Ottoline Morrell. I couldn't get beyond riffling the chapters. The personages Lawrence made have remained with me all my life; the once-living woman of flesh and blood is of no interest, vis-à-vis *Women in Love,* disappeared into whatever fiction she may have suggested to the writer.

Yet the game persists. The I-spy includes as prey the writer her- or himself.

What is it these impertinent interrogators want from us, the writers?

An admission that your Albertine was actually gay Albert? That Malone was Beckett's neglected grandfather? That Nabokov alias Humbert Humbert didn't chase only butterflies?

The writer has to recognize that the guessing-game, the prying and prurience and often absurdity, is merely a vulgar expression of a mystery that the relation of fiction to the appearance of reality is, to those who are not writers. And because that relation is part mystery to writers themselves, and what we do know we fully expect to be disbelieved or mis-construed—you have to be a performer of the mystery to understand it, as has been said of love-making—we are offended by the crass approach of curiosity and turn aside the presumptive question with a flat denial.

No—so-and-so is not you-think-you-know-who; then where has he come from? Is he, so life-like, supposed to be some sort of ectoplasm foaming from the writer?

Which is what we writers imply when we snap back that he is *imaginary*.

It is beyond dispute that no character in fiction, even if conceived as an ape, a beetle, a phantasm, is without connection with real persons experienced by the writer within contact of sight, sound and touch, or second-hand through experience recorded by others in one medium or another, and whether or not the writer is always aware of this.

As a typology is created through the superimposition of transparencies of many individuals so that the features that recur predominantly become the identikit, so for the individual fictional character—the very antithesis of a typological collective—the writer selects and mixes *differences* in what the roving imagination seizes upon to its purpose.

That is the half-truth that makes the denial a half-lie.

For this creature formed from the material and immaterial— what has breathed upon the writer intimately, brushed by him in the street, and the ideas that shape behaviour in his personal consciousness of his time and place, directing the flesh in action—this fictional creature is brought into the synthesis of being by the writer's imagination alone, is not cloned from some nameable Adam's rib or Eve's womb. Imagined: yes. Taken from life: yes.

What do we writers have to work on as looters in that fragmentation of the possibilities of observation, of interaction,

4

of grasp, in the seen and unseen, constant flux and reflux, the conscious and unconscious defined as 'life'?

Even if one wanted to replicate, there is no seeing, knowing, the depth and whole of anyone, and therefore no possibility of so-and-so *being* you-know-who, even if someone's prepared to sue to assert this. Damages may be gained because of ugly motives or actions attributed by the author to a fictional character that the complainant avers is himself or herself; the odd fact is that the acceptable characteristics by which the complainant *chooses* to identify himself with the personage are no less fictional than the ones that are *rejected* as untrue and offensive. Of course, no libel law recognizes this . . .

The writer in relation to real personages is more like Primo Levi's metamir, which, 'a metaphysical mirror, does not obey the law of optics but reproduces your image *as it is seen by the person who stands before you*' (my italics).

This comes to me as one of the closest definitions of the process of the imagination upon actuality.

The writer is that person who stands before you.

What he or she finds in the individual is not a working model to be dragged off and wired up to a book but a series of intimations the individual does not present to the ordinary mirror of the world.

Of these flashes—an always incomplete series of *what the individual is* (for the metamir image receives what she is *not* saying as she speaks, the anger in his eyes that *belies* his smile, the *echo* in her silences, the gagged messages signalled by gestures; what the writer remembers of *him* from a previous encounter, has heard recounted of *her* by others, etcetera)—of these flashes the writer retains one or two, perhaps, for future

5

use in the personality of a quite different personage. For one of the few sure things the writer knows is that inconsistency is the consistency of human character.

There simply is not enough *there,* of what can be grasped in a single individual to make a fictional character.

To be 'life-like' a character always must be *larger than life,* more intense, compounded and condensed in essence of personality than could exist materially. The abstract medium of the printed page must be overcome. The fragments of ultraperceptive knowledge are stowed away in the facility for which 'filing system' as a convenient description will not do, because what the writer has within is a system that is both storing and working on, at the same time, material that is being added to, often over years.

This is more than memory; memory is random, does not categorize.

This facility or faculty means that the images of the metamir are collected, here, there, at intervals or in a sudden rush, and some day transformed by the writer into one of his characters, called up in imagination in answer to a theme or giving rise to one.

If writers need justify this subconscious process morally— although we assert the right to have no tendentious purpose, no message, the right to declare with Ibsen that 'a book is not about, it *is*'—we lack no means to do so.

Graham Greene has a snooty Olympian answer on his existential journey: 'When I came to write I was handing out alternative destinies to real people whom I had encountered.'

For Joseph Conrad what the writer does is 'rescue work carried out in darkness . . . this snatching of vanished phases of turbulence.' 'What is a novel,' he asks, 'if not a conviction of

❧

our fellow-men's existence strong enough to take upon itself a form of imagined life clearer than reality.'

❧

In my own life as a writer I have had the strange experience of pre-empting the moves of the prying game.

In the 1970s I wrote a novel in which one of the central characters was a revolutionary hero. It was unique in my fiction in that it did have an element of the tendentious—it was, for me, something of a coded homage paid to such a man, an anti-apartheid activist, who had died serving a life sentence, his ashes withheld from his daughters by the prison authorities of the day.

As a clue to this homage, as well as for the purposes of using the authentic rhetoric of the time for the public statements of my character, I did something I had never done before and have not done since: I reproduced an existing document, part of the speech made in court by an actual personage, a South African Communist, when he was sentenced to life imprisonment.

There was an additional complication, by the way: the publication of the words of a convicted prisoner, whether Communist or not, alive or dead, was then a treasonable offence under the law of my country.

I had known the man and his family, and had been awedly fascinated by the extraordinary condition of danger and self-discipline in what was openly evidenced as their close-knit life. I was not a casual acquaintance but had been by no means an intimate in their house, neither, although I was committed to the Left, was I a member of the revolutionary group which was more than their home.

7

I was the metamir standing before them.

The novel itself found its opening paragraphs from a single moment like that; I was waiting outside a prison to visit a friend detained for political interrogation, and there was the schoolgirl daughter of the man, presented to me, as it were, in the group of prison visitors, that strange assembly in whom social association is reduced to connection with the outcast: the offenders against the edicts of the social order, criminal or political, indiscriminately put behind bars.

What was she thinking?

What was her sense of a family obligation that *chose for her* to stand there among the relatives of thieves and murderers?

She was in gym frock and blazer of a conventional private school for young ladies; how did her genteel bourgeois teachers and classmates receive a girl whose father was in prison for treason against the State that protected their white privilege?

Of course, the writer in me quickly eclipsed the renderer of homage.

From that mystery, the facility that works upon while it stores fragments of perception, the snatched phases of turbulence that is existence both lived and observed by the writer, came the alternative lives of the man and the schoolgirl, created in the imagination but touching, here and there, perforce, the actual, since these imaginary lives, by the nature of my story, were contained in time by aleatory real events of politics and history.

An act of homage, just as well as any other, can be construed by curiosity as proof that so-and-so surely is you-know-who. Although my novel—to adapt Piaget's definition of the history of intelligence—was not an 'inventory of elements' that homage per se is limited to be, but the 'bundle of transformations' he cites in opposition, I knew that the guessing-game would buzz over the published book.

The fact that I as surely knew it would be banned because of the points at which it was anchored to real events of out-lawed political movements, from liberal to left, bothered me less. Bans, along with the governments that impose them, do not last forever. (And indeed, the novel was both banned and eventually released.)

But the effect that the guessing-game might have on the schoolgirl, now adult, subject to it, who would remember my presence in hers outside the prison that day, concerned me.

Her father's name certainly would be attached to my fictional character; the persona I had created in place of her father would be attributed to him. The complex family relations I had created would be attributed to her and her family. The ontological conflicts within unquestioned political faith imposed by parents upon children with the rigour of a religious one would be seen as their own conflicts.

Worst of all, for the novelist: would the girl's finding be that *I had understood nothing;* that the metamir had failed to discover what the silver-backed mirror of the apparent cannot reveal?

So in place of waiting for the question to be thrust at her as well as at me, I sent my answer. I sent her the manuscript of the novel before publication, before anyone else had read it. With it I enclosed a letter. I have kept that letter for fifteen years. It has been my secret, and I open it here because I suppose it belongs, at least, in this discourse as one writer's answer, in respect of fiction, to the mystery behind the ignorant superficiality of the guessing-game.

I began with the proposition that this was the strangest letter I should ever write and might be the strangest she would ever receive. I told her that for the present the novel was hers and mine; only she and I, as she read it, knew of its contents.

But I was a writer and it was meant to be, would be, read

9

by whoever wished to do so; soon it would be open to anyone. Even if it were to be banned in our own country it would be read elsewhere.

Then people would come to her and say, This is your father, this is you, as they would come to me and say, This is so-and-so, this is his daughter. She had to be the first to read the fiction because she would be the one to know, as they never could know, that although the man lived for the same political convictions and human ideals and suffered for them the same imprisonment and death as her father, he was not her father, could not be.

I could not 'know', have known, her father in the private and personal moments that became the dimensions of my character, I could not have 'known' the hidden motives behind the public interactions I observed performed, and the interactions I was privy to, occasionally a bit player in, his relations with his family, political comrades and friends.

I could not have known the clandestine connections that must have existed between hidden cause and observable effect in many of the events staged in her family's life that were apparently inexplicable.

I could not have known what sort of arcane curriculum of parental love (for it had been clear to me in my contact with the family that the father was a loving and loved one) allowed the grim determinism of a way of life that inevitably would land a tender schoolgirl outside prison gates as if she merely had been sent down to the local shops.

I had a critical as well as a hagiographical conviction of her father's and her existence strong enough to take on a form of imagined life. I was aware of the risk that the conditioning of my own subconscious—that conditioning to which I had been subjected by the conjunction of apartheid and capitalism in the formation of ideas about personal Communist mores—might distort that conviction.

I had made my snatch of the phases of turbulence of that existence I shared with them in a particular country in a particular era. In the vision of the metamir I had invented alternative being.

I explained to her that this was why, during the four years I was writing the novel, I had avoided contact with her and other surviving members of the family. I deliberately had allowed friendship to lapse. Perhaps it seems naïve, perhaps it was my quaint notion of authorial morality, perhaps it was my eccentric methodology—I had the idea that there must be no evidence, in the test of creation, that I was 'studying' her in order to inform my fictions, measuring the progression of her life in the to-and-fro of past and present that delineates personality.

Before I left her to the novel itself, I concluded my letter by reminding her that although the I-spy game would be played and might disturb her, the players could be positing only yet another alternative—to mine, yes—an alternative life for her and her father, her family; they could not touch what she knew to have been their own.

There was silence from her for several weeks.

Strangely, although I had been fearfully apprehensive about giving her the manuscipt to read, I was tranquil. It was as if the three of us, the schoolgirl waiting to visit her father in prison, my fictional character and I, together had a dimension of immaterial existence to be privately occupied for a while.

This is easier to write than to say. I have always thought bunkum the coy romantic claim of some writers that their characters take over, write themselves, etcetera. It was nothing

11

like that. The temporal and the eternal, Lukács's duality of inwardness and the outside world, between which a writer is always precariously spreadeagled, attained an equilibrium. Life and fiction became whole.

One afternoon she walked through my gate carrying the manuscript.

So that was what it was, after all, a package of paper; we sat and exchanged the usual generalities and then, in a gap, there it was between us, the novel.

She said, 'This was our life.'

And nothing more.

I knew this was the best response I should ever have to that novel. Perhaps the best I should ever have in respect of any of my fictions. Something I should never receive again.

No critic's laudation could match it; no critic's damning could destroy it.

For she was not speaking of verisimilitude, she was not matching mug-shots, she knew that facts, events, sequences were not so; she was conceding that while no one can have total access to the lives of others—not even through means of the analyst's case-book, the biographer's research, the subjectively-composed revelations of diaries and letters—by contrast, on her or his vision the novelist may receive, from the ethos those lives give off, a vapour of the truth condensed, in which, a finger tracing upon a window-pane, the story may be written.

Milan Kundera once told an interviewer 'there is a limit beyond which the novelist can theorize no further on his own novels and whence he must know how to keep his silence.'

I have reached that limit.

I turn away to a perception of the origin of character in fiction less subjective in the person of the inquirer but even more subjective in the sense of the interpretation.

By this I mean where the thesis is not that of a writer defending his own work from the charge of predatory realism, but of a literary critic studying that writer's work on the premise that not someone else's filched life but the writer's own is the story—the *work itself* is totally subjective.

I take as example a study by Edward W. Said, since with its title, *Joseph Conrad and the Fiction of Autobiography,* he boldly stakes this premise.

Here he sees the novel as essentially 'a discrete analogy of the mechanism' of the writer's life, mainly on the evidence of the writer's letters. 'To put forth the secret of one's imagination,' Said says, 'is not to enact a religious event, but to perform a religious rite; that is, the rite implies but withholds the actual event.'

So far, no novelist could have formulated more elegantly a remarkable definition of the ontological relation of fiction to reality. But the conclusion that follows does not 'withhold the actual event' at all: I quote: 'In this manner the life of the novelist *in its totality* is given the episodic structure which, while not revealing the whole of the writer's life, is a discrete analogy of the mechanism of that life. To the reader this can be made intelligible through the action (or plot) of a fictional work' (my italics).

Broken up piecemeal or not, mechanism or not, the author's life is the 'actual event' of the making of the book. On this premise, not only is the writer embalmed in his own words, his work is seen as determined by the limits of his own life. Every man his metamir.

❧

Of course, there are distinguished examples of this as a matter of *own choice:* the writers who are deliberately self-obsessed, genuinely finding revelation for us in the couplings of their own physical- and thought-processes as certain creatures are equipped with male genitalia at one end of their bodies and female genitalia at the other, so that they may perform a complete life-cycle in themselves.

But to posit that the writer's range of imagination plays solely or mainly upon his own life, that the writer is imprisoned in the need to 'make this intelligible', that fiction is autobiography, is to deny the secret of the imagination, not to put it forth.

Beside the proposition I would place Toni Morrison's statement: 'The ability of writers to imagine what is not the self . . . is the test of their power'; and Lukács's axiom of the writer's great unrealizable aim of encompassing, out of life's manifestations, the totality that 'is the only method capable of understanding and reproducing reality.'

Said says, for Conrad 'writing and life were . . . struggles to win over and then claim unknown ground. His personal struggle Conrad saw reflected in the political and historical developments around him.'

Does the high aim of creativity in the first statement imply that the second means Conrad conceived of himself as Lukács's world-historical figure in the person of his characters, that—as Said concludes—Conrad was Lord Jim, was Marlow, was even the unfortunately named Nigger of the Narcissus?

I call up the von Trottas of Joseph Roth's *Radetzky March* and *The Emperor's Tomb:* how far removed they are from the autobiography of Roth as wandering Jewish exile, while embodying completely the history that made and destroyed him, a world in dissolution.

14

❦

One would have to accept that Conrad reduced the splendid magnification with which he gazed over the ocean of life down to a focus closed on the miniature self; that he did this rather than followed, as writers must in their work, the trajectory of their own lives through peopled history as an inescapable element in sensibility, rather than receive history as a reflection of self: that so great a writer has to be believed to be so least inventive. Even promoted to the highest level of literary analysis, this comes close to literature as therapy, character as authorial catharsis.

❦

The writer is the Adam's rib of character.

The writer's life is the story, according to Edward Said.

'What is told is the telling', not the subject, not the plot, not a transformation of the writer's life, according to Roland Barthes.

There are no characters at all.

Yet the two, Said and Barthes, may have been thinking and working towards these opposed theses of literary determinism in the same decade, since Said's *Joseph Conrad and the Fiction of Autobiography* was published in 1966 and Barthes's *S/Z* in 1970.

I speak of 'theses' and not 'conclusions' because the disagreements about what fiction is, where it comes from—a coherence in the babble of the conscious and unconscious, a gathering from a diaspora that does not know from what territory of cognition it has been dispersed?—of course continue and must continue.

Critical theorists themselves shift or move on in their perceptions.

In his recent superb study *Culture and Imperialism* Said sees

15

Conrad's writings as central to the exposure of culture's partnership with imperialism in the nineteenth century, rather than as an exposition of self as fictional character.

Barthes, late in his life, found the meaning of it not in the telling, but nostalgically in that life as plot, himself as subject.

But the two early books remain in our literary canon, their theses representative of at least two of the sand-shoals of literary theory that wash up on either bank of the writer's imagination as it flows unconcernedly on.

The writer *is* the fiction; the writer is dismissed from the fiction.

In the one, the guessing-game turns with scholarly licence to the author as character, definitive prototype.

In the other, the author is simply not there. For that marvellous piece of entertainment, Roland Barthes's *S/Z*, does not seek Balzac in Balzac's story 'Sarrasine.'

The Proairetisms, the Semes, the Cultural Codes, the Hermeneutisms do not refer to autobiography. While, according to Barthes, 'to interpret a text' is to 'appreciate what *plural* constitutes it,' the author, the compiler, is not present in that plural. He is not consulted.

As for the origin of character outside the model of the author, the old castrato in Balzac's story is 'semantic space': the reading of the 'realistic portrait' is not even attributable to the author, it is 'a cubist reading . . . piled up, altered, juxtaposed' by signifieds the author, assumedly, is not aware of. It is the reader who is the 'producer of the text'; the writer is the labourer, wheeling barrowloads of words for an edifice of which only the 'writerly' reader-cum-critic knows the grand design.

16

❧

Although one would not want to be without this classic of semiology in which the author, Barthes, is himself so enchantingly present, for me there is a recoil from Richard Howard's enthusiastic conclusion of his introduction to the English translation of *S/Z:* He asks: 'can we ever again read Balzac *in all innocence?* can we ever want to?'

The answer is a resounding 'Yes!' We do.

We can read Balzac without voice-over. We may find pleasure and illumination in his characters and his 'readerly' text— that is, in Barthean view, one that accepts as givens the intentions of the author as stated in the text according to the author's own understanding of what he is doing with words— without the interruption of the 'writerly' text's divagations.

Further, what the writerly text inexplicably ignores is that there is a personal hermeneutics in the act of reading. *Every* reading is 'writerly' by this definition. Every intelligent reader has her or his life-contextual Proairetisms, Semes, Cultural Codes.

Some basic signifiers are shared by us all, but most are individual. The antithesis of the flower-like beauty of women and the 'leprous gray' of the old castrato, together in a room in Balzac's story, may provide the same signifiers to all readers, out of a common experience of human blooming and decay. But the lexia 'Midnight had just sounded from the clock of the Elysée-Bourbon' is unlikely to have the same signifiers, if any 'writerly' one beyond passing time announced by twelve chimes, for a reader who has never walked through the streets of old Paris, is shaky in French political and social history, is not aware of the fluctuations on the Bourse in the period, and has not followed the adventures of a Lucien de Rubempré.

The lexia will not signify in the gnomic code, as it does for Barthes, as follows: 'A metonymy leads from the Elysée-Bourbon to the seme *wealth,* since the Faubourg Saint-Honoré is a wealthy neighbourhood. This wealth is itself connoted: a neighbourhood of *nouveaux-riches,* the Faubourg Saint-Honoré refers by synecdoche to the Paris of the Bourbon Restoration, a mythic place of sudden fortunes whose origins are suspect; where gold is produced without an origin, diabolically (the symbol of speculation)'.

'Words are symbols that assume a shared memory,' Borges says. That other polymath, Barthes, has the aristocrat-of-the-intellect's innocent assumption that every writerly reader shares the signifiers of Barthes's own culture. Let us eat his cake . . .

If the author is not responsible for his fictions, if *he is not there,* it is certainly also questionable whether the 'plural' that constitutes them can be composed in the hermeneutics of one individual for all of us.

If, on the other hand, the author is *the only one there,* himself his own characters, his experience the matched source of all his fictions, there is no space in literature for the diversity of humankind with its wild contradictions of the nature of existence.

It is surely the morality of fiction that is being questioned by those who accuse the writer of looting the character of living personages.

It is the creative authority of the writer that is being questioned when the reader is made producer of the text.

Both are part of the permanent inquiry into the sources of the imagination. Somewhere between, the two extremes, fiction as an *enactment of life,* character as its imaginatively embodied discourse, keep their half-secrets, even from us, the practitioners, writers themselves, leaving us half-lying, half-attempting the truth in telling—so far as we consciously know—how we think we create.

Which is what I have tried my hand at here.

Not so much to contest that of others, my attempt has been made in the spirit of Frank Kermode's words, 'to use fiction for its true purpose, the discovery and registration of the human world.'

2

HANGING ON A SUNRISE
TESTIMONY AND THE IMAGINATION IN
REVOLUTIONARY WRITINGS

In the early Seventies, when I was preparing a small book on African writing, I found it necessary and justified, as a canon of criticism, to make a qualitative distinction between testimony and imaginative writing in what was indiscriminately accepted as post-modern in literature. If this raises an eyebrow among those, including myself, who distrust the arbitrary of high and low and grant literature the widest definition, I nevertheless find something of my definition of the Seventies renewably valid in the cultural history of the present and immediate past in my country, South Africa.

What I wrote twenty years ago about what was coming out of Africa in general, I now see as applicable, if rather differently, confined to my own country. I quote myself: 'Are we approaching it [the writing] as testimony of social change, or as literature? In the first category, *anything* literate is of interest, and justifies publication and study. In the second, the creative gifts or lack of them, of the writer, are what matters . . . If you

❧

want to read the facts of the retreat from Moscow in 1815, you may read a history book; if you want to know what war is like and how people of a certain time and background dealt with it as their personal situation, you must read *War and Peace*.'

Under conditions of life in the long apartheid era in South Africa much was not spoken, much was not written. It was not only the ninety-plus categories of offence decreed by the censorship laws that silenced people. Those who were actively engaged in an experience just as characteristic of the time as that of oppression—the experience of revolutionary action—were silenced by the necessity for secrecy; for by the thread of an ill-considered word might hang a life—the speaker's, the writer's, or that of another.

No one thus engaged could give an account of actions or thoughts that were, in fact, to be the definitive experience of the time if we grant that the order of experience that anticipates and is carried over to form the future is the definitive one; an experience which should be set up against what is generally perceived as the Age of Apartheid. Those years were equally the Age of Revolution.

Those of us who were outside the revolutionary movement or on its fringes were not only unaware of what men and women deep within it were doing; not only could not know the personal conflicts and difficult moral decisions involved in their actions, but often, out of lack of such knowledge, were unable to understand the significance of certain behaviour patterns, quirks of demeanour, in otherwise familiar people. Nothing could be asked; nothing could be explained. Only in the great treason trials of the era were the explanations of some of these matters disjointedly bared in flashes of confession extracted by the horrors of interrogation.

I remember a visit from a woman whose daughter had been

21

detained; she wanted me to intercede with the Security Police (a pathetic plea; as if I could have any possible influence there!) because she was convinced that her daughter had nothing to do with revolutionary activity, she was 'innocent.' When the girl was brought to trial it was clear that she was an active revolutionary and proud to be so; if not 'innocent', then not guilty of standing by indifferent to the misery of others. She had maintained the 'innocent' facade in order to protect her family; to harbour a political activist, even your own daughter, was to be an accessory to treason, and frequently led to detention.

With the amnesty for political prisoners, and for exiles who had a price on their heads, much of what was unknown to the public, much obfuscated by rumour and distorted by the apartheid regime's demonization of individuals for political scare tactics may be, is being, told.

Personal testimony is piecing together the chronicle of an era torn apart by silencing decrees, which without this witness would remain blown about in the gutters of time. This is not so much an alternative history as a gathering-in of what was missing in South Africans' *perception* of their country, the actual context of their lives.

Back in the Seventies, I was using 'testimony' in the sense of a value-judgment of works of fiction that were *no more than testimony:* lacked the transforming imaginative dimension, dealt with the surface reality of experience, often in the form of thinly-disguised autobiography.

I was concerned that the criteria of exploration of the possibilities of language, the power of insight to human behaviour beneath its outward manifestation, the unending expedition into the mystery of existence, the creation of a world of words that, for me, distinguishes literature from testimony—the ways of telling from the tale told—would be debased by acceptance of mere disguised testimony as imaginative literature.

My present approach to testimony is different.

This testimony makes no pretension to be fiction. Indeed its purpose is quite the reverse. It is witness—validated by being given by each in his person on his own responsibility—to actions, events, ideological positions, and mores performed, enjoined, held and upheld by that individual. There have been too many necessities for evasion and disguise; this testimony is the liberation of openness.

Even in the context of literary quality in which I questioned testimony twenty years ago, I recognized testimony's intrinsic value. In the much-quoted words of Milan Kundera, 'The struggle of man against power is the struggle of memory against forgetting.' Testimony is the agent of that struggle. But testimony in my country today is not only provision against forgetting what we knew; it is also the provision of what we never knew.

During the Age of Apartheid there was, of course, the emergence of prison testimony in the form of books such as Ruth First's *117 Days,* Albie Sachs's *Jail Diary of Albie Sachs,* Hugh Lewin's *Bandiet,* D. M. Zwelonke's *Robben Island.* Most were banned—a few copies smuggled from abroad reached a small number of South African readers—until in the Eighties they began to emerge from the political obsolescence of the censorship laws, which were rapidly being overtaken by events in the streets and townships.

Valuable as these testimonies are to the completion of our political and social history, they did not, could not provide a chronicle of Underground activity. As this was still in progress

23

nothing could be so much as mentioned, neither name nor event, that might lead the Security Police to activists still at what passed for liberty—a constant surveillance.

The writings appearing now need have no such inhibitions.

And the urgency with which the missing past needs to be restored by living memory against forgetting is emphasized by another fact of life for activists under the old regime: documents, diaries, love-letters—all were destroyed in order not to leave a paper trail, or were seized in police raids. The archive of the time rests in Security Police files; or did: the hungry jaws of the shredder were kept busy during the months leading up to South Africa's first democratic election and the installation of the government of national unity in 1994.

In the six months preceding the election I attended the launches of two works written by revolutionary activists. Each party itself was a phenomenon I had thought I should never live to see in South Africa. The wine glasses balanced in the crush of black and white people, the sociable chatter, the fanned-out display of the book, and the author beaming embarrassedly in conventional manner—the one, an exile whose photograph was for two decades banned from publication in any newspaper; the other, an ex-prisoner convicted of treason. The occasion for celebration went far beyond the launch of a book. With this sense I took the books home. Reading them, I found my old preoccupation with the relation of testimony to literature returning.

'To write is to sit in judgment on oneself,' said Ibsen. He might have been commenting on the character of these—and perhaps all—testimonies. In my context, beside this dictum one might set Büchner's: 'Terror is the outgrowth of virtue'—the virtue of revolt against oppression.

Both writers of the books I brought home from the launching parties were declared terrorists by the apartheid regime and accepted as such by many people who were nominally against the regime; liberalism being the middle class of politics, where both the Underdog, revolution, and the Oppressor, the status quo, are equally condemned. And both men, in the nature of their testimony, provide evidence of their actions as an outgrowth of virtue—'virtue' to stand for a different base in each: the one, Carl Niehaus, a devout Christian; the other, Ronnie Kasrils, a Jewish non-believer humanist-cum-Marxist. From this aspect, their writings sit in judgment on themselves as well as on the regime both came to oppose with revolutionary action.

'Armed and Dangerous': My Underground Struggle against Apartheid is the title of Ronnie Kasrils's book. A fanfare characteristic of a man to whom flamboyance is germane as fire-breathing to a dragon.

The dragon's spectacular exhalation is mythical; that is why I choose it as analogous to Kasrils's style as a man: in his book he presents himself as a personality become a mythic figure: classic—the young Don Juan; and contemporary—he accepts with obvious exuberance the newspapers' dubbing him the 'Red Pimpernel' when, in various disguises, he evaded arrest. He is even able to mock while boasting. It was the Security Police who, indeed, provided him with the title of his book; on his last run Underground they published a warning to the public that Kasrils was 'armed and dangerous.' Meanwhile, unarmed except for a beard and a baseball cap, he was slipping out of hiding to attend his passion—football matches, breezily calculating that this sort of public event was the last at which he would be looked for.

He tells his story—except for the final chapters—on the model of a popular adventure novel or a Hitchcock movie, and somehow, by making it entertaining, makes it seem less testimonial rather than more literary.

In melodramatic opening pages he leaves England to enter South Africa after twenty-seven years of exile, 'watched from the shadows' by 'unnamed accomplices.' This unspecific image (he certainly could name them now), debased for us outsiders by overuse in banal contexts, conveys less as the verity of revolutionary experience than a practical description he gives of exactly how he learned to make an explosive device with a condom as part of the fuse. The time the condom takes to disintegrate can be calculated exactly, in order for the individual who has set the device to get clear.

The solution—truly a paradigm of the Absurd—is a revelation of the mundane by which a revolution proceeds; just as Kasrils's romanticism does not mean that he was not a totally serious and dedicated revolutionary. And a brave man, since I believe that willingness to risk your own life, as he has done again and again, may claim to be a moral position in pursuance of a just cause by means which include violence.

Kasrils comes from a poor immigrant Jewish family settled in Johannesburg, and out of his own experience in the streets and as a humble employee became drawn to working-class issues.

This meant, of course, the position of blacks—their low wages, the restriction on the levels of skills they might acquire and on their free movement to sell their labour where they wished. With the zest with which he seems to have done

26

everything in his life, he took part in political protest on broader issues of political power and found that the South African Communist Party offered the kind of non-racial action he thought most effective. He did not enter the Party by way of Marx, Lenin and Luxemburg; the theory in accordance with which the actions were taken came later, with reading. Although obviously extremely intelligent, he does not emerge with the self-doubts and inner conflicts of an intellectual but reveals himself as a quick-minded pragmatist with ideological motivation arising from the urgency of a sense of injustice *that must find its solution.*

The Soviet Union was for decades virtually the only country that offered concrete support—money and military training— to both the South African Communist Party and the African National Congress in the struggle against apartheid, while the United States and Britain satisfied their consciences with pious verbal condemnation of racism, at the same time supporting successive apartheid governments. From the Party, Kasrils joined the armed wing of the African National Congress, Umkhonto we Sizwe (Spear of the Nation), and went for military training to Odessa.

Many blacks and some whites, men and women, were in exile in the Soviet Union during the Fifties, Sixties and Seventies, but none has written of experience there in a personal way, as Kasrils does. The first testimony comes from him. With honest hindsight—if only in passing during his narrative—while he describes an agreeable life of comfort and friendship he admits that this was enjoyed as a privilege, and that in his concentration on the cause for whose pursuance he was preparing himself, he was naïve: he was not particularly aware that conditions were much different for the average Russian.

Based back in Africa in one African country or another outside South Africa's borders, Kasrils rose to become Head of Military Intelligence in MK—Umkhonto we Sizwe.

In South Africa, we knew of him only in the headline persona of 'Mastermind' of the blowing up of an oil installation, or—on his secret forays into the country and out again—the infamous 'Red Pimpernel.' Home legally now, and no less than Deputy Minister of Defence in our first democratically elected, non-racial government, his testimony provides a dimension of the life of a fellow South African that was unknown and unimagined but that, nevertheless, belongs to us; what we have been and are.

Kasrils not only infiltrated South Africa to organize underground activity; he was one of the few white men in Umkhonto we Sizwe's guerrilla forces fighting the South African army in the wilderness and desert. This brotherhood-in-arms earns an acceptance, now, from blacks, whose depth cannot be reached by whites in any other form of commitment to black liberation, even if that commitment was attained by other kinds of personal risk.

As for whites, Kasrils lived in the bush as an MK soldier; the testimony inevitably invites armchair-and-protest-march activists to judge themselves by comparison. The experience of what passed for peace in South Africa—in which whites were safe while blacks suffered daily the cruelty and violence associated with wars—let alone the actual experience of guerrilla war from which armchair judgment was far removed, meant that even staunch anti-apartheid supporters among whites were horrified, revolted by the evidence of torture employed by certain African National Congress commanders. This was perpetrated at a detention camp in Tanzania for South African government spies who had infiltrated Umkhonto we Sizwe ranks. Kasrils con-

demns what happened but points out how the attitude of those
who had greatly suffered at the hands of the South African
government differed almost beyond understanding from that of
people who had not. 'The question about how to contain and
punish enemy agents had become a serious problem by the
1980s. Many MK cadres had a similar attitude to the people at
home. Spies and traitors did not deserve to live.'

It was right to be horrified. It was easy to condemn.

One of the values of such testimony becoming available now
is that it brings this re-examination of moral positions and calls
into question the self-justification of the limits most of us made
to the extent to which we were prepared—or able—to muster
courage to oppose an evil regime which we *declared* we wholly
condemned. Testimony creates the conditions for reflection. It
is a re-examination of the past to which, whether or not we
were direct protagonists, we all find ourselves subject.

Ambiguity in our very conceptions of courage, for example,
became clear some time after Kasrils's return to South Africa
under amnesty.

There was supposedly free political activity by then, but the
assembly at an African National Congress rally was forbidden
to leave a stadium and march to the village of Bisho to demand
political rights in Ciskei, one of apartheid's ethnic 'homelands'
to which millions of black South Africans were confined in
poverty.

All demonstrators present were unarmed. Kasrils led a break
through barriers in defiance of the order. A number of those
who streamed out with him were shot dead, without warning,
by the surrounding police force. The fact that he risked his own
life to assert a right did not shield him from public criticism of
reckless exposure of the lives of others.

A concept flips over; the courage of a man like Kasrils is

perceived instead as foolhardiness; what makes him a hero in the field makes him a dangerous adventurer in civil life.

And the question is opened: how much do we South Africans know of the revolutionary personality which was formed by, arose in, and belongs to our society, its inheritance? Did we not, through failure to end apartheid by other means, send those people out through the barriers? While not, unlike Kasrils, ourselves baring our breasts to the bullets?

Aside from explaining his naivety in the Soviet Union years, Kasrils's testimony does not consciously sit in judgment on himself until the last chapter of his book, where he sets out, complete with diagrams of the Bisho stadium and police action, his personal vindication of what he did there. For the rest, he appears as a man without self-doubt, in no conflict over ends and means, at peace with himself in a warring life of necessity.

If both Ronnie Kasrils and Carl Niehaus arrived at the life of a revolutionary in the same cause, the liberation of the people of South Africa from racism, they reached it by different stations. The outgrowth was from different perceptions of virtue.

Kasrils moved to revolutionary action through the stations of humanism and Marxism, virtually untrammelled by ties of any opposing family or societal counter-ethic or tradition. His immigrant family had no roots in South Africa; he put down his own in the cause of the black majority. He evidently felt no pull of the option to shelter himself, as a white man, in the white minority's fenced garden.

Carl Niehaus comes from a devoutly Christian Afrikaner family with an ancestry on the land that goes back far enough into the years of early white settlement for their line to have woven a social textile in a tight pattern of beliefs, ethics and tradition based on the Dutch Reformed Church.

At an early age he came to the dichotomy he formulates in the mode of his present testimony: '"They" are members of the Afrikaner farming communities of Groot Marico and Schuinsdrift in the Western Transvaal. These are stalwart people, lovers of the soil. "They" are my uncles and aunts and cousins—my own people. "We" are the people who spend our nights in meetings or hunched over our computers, contemplating the future. Us and them—all belonging to one country, grappling with our fears, working for the right to hope.'

And he takes, as the title of his autobiographical testimony, his manner of asserting that right. *Fighting for Hope:* the simple directness of the title holds—the sweet pulp of uplift surrounding a kernel of desperate honesty—the conflict contained in the lines I have quoted.

This apposition as opposition has accompanied him through his life as a revolutionary. His testimony is essentially of the moral agony of being at the same time *both* 'Us' and 'Them', an existential position which has been one of the phenomena of the divisions of successive racist regimes in a country that made us what we are.

Outraging his family by joining the African National Congress, Niehaus nevertheless never ceased to feel himself part of those 'stalwart people' whose regime he was acting to destroy.

Becoming one of those who spent their nights in meetings planning sabotage, he continued in unshaken belief in the religion of those people. 'In times of struggle or conflict' he continued 'to pray to and follow the norms laid down by God . . . In times of suffering and loss I pray to the God of love and forgiveness.'

31

He posits the unthinkably difficult position of loving his people while hating what they stood for. For him, the moral centre of self cannot be secured, as for Kasrils, alone by the moral code of a cause; for him, still, 'The danger of losing oneself lies in forgetting one's origins.'

The painful division between the 'Us' of the Afrikaner working-class community to which he belonged and the 'Them' of revolt against the regime came to him when as a schoolboy in 1976 he was issued with a cadet's rifle as protection against an anticipated attack by blacks on white schools.

'My own excitement was mixed with uncertainty . . . *Could* I actually shoot someone?' He remembered the day when going with his parents' church group to help run a Bible class in a black hostel he realized that 'the filthy compound was a place where real people were living.' He wondered 'whether what was happening in Soweto was an explosion of pent-up anger and frustration because they refused to endure those conditions any longer.' But he had been taught that the State represents the will of God: 'surely Mr Potgieter [the headmaster] had the right to hand out rifles to protect the State's God-given authority?'

Yet 'whenever I managed to draw a perfectly straight mental line from the will of God to the authority of the State, I saw those workers; sitting so silently on their paraffin tins, listening to the recorded sermon.'

During the school break he went into one of the toilets and closed the door. 'Amidst the sounds of boys urinating and the sharp smell of urine, I kneeled with my elbows on the porcelain seat and prayed. Please God, help me make the right choice . . .' He refused to stand armed guard. 'I knew that I would be mocked and called a coward, which was exactly what happened.'

❧

It was the choice of his life.

It was an adolescent's humble preview of the decision he would make to become active in the Underground of the African National Congress, wrestling with his conscience over the theory of a just war—God versus the State, the hostel dwellers versus the headmaster, once again—where violence could be used only as a last resort. He

> was convinced that the African National Congress had met this requirement, but . . . I had to be sure that the armed struggle was being directed at the government and industrial targets only, with a minimum of loss of life among civilians. I was white and privileged and had never been at the receiving end of apartheid, which is probably why it took me so long to make a final decision. If the government had expropriated my grandfather's farm [the implication is a parallel with the forced removals of blacks from their land], which he had bought with his hard-earned mineworker's wages, would he not have resorted to violence? . . . For me, the time of vacillation was over; I had to commit myself . . . once and for all.

He had been expelled from an Afrikaans university for putting up forbidden posters calling for the release of Nelson Mandela, and similar sins. Now the African National Congress entrusted him with the task of identifying selective targets for sabotage; he had committed himself to violence.

There were plans to disrupt municipal services, electricity supplies. But for him there is always revealed the anxiety—unrevolutionary scruples not known to a Kasrils—of the Us and Them dwelling inside him: 'I was worried that my lack of technical knowledge would prevent me from making a correct evaluation . . . If it were possible to disrupt the electricity supply, how would this affect hospitals and intensive care units?'

33

For advice on these matters he depended on a man who betrayed him. Reconnoitring a gas-works one night, he walked into the glare of a Security Police trap; he and his girl-friend were arrested in their apartment soon after.

Andrzej Wajda had Danton declare, in the film *Danton's Death:* 'Haven't you understood that we had to allow ourselves to be imprisoned? In order to open the eyes of the people?' When brought to trial for treason, Niehaus and his girl-friend, Jansie, refused their counsel's advice to plead guilty in order to get a lighter sentence 'because we had not betrayed our country and its people'.

He was sentenced to fifteen years' imprisonment, she to four. In the course of serving these sentences they were offered early release on conditions which stipulated they could not take any further part in political activity. Again, they refused, although he was taunted with lying statements that his wife—they had married in prison, while incarcerated separately—had accepted release.

He testifies to this last of the many stations of moral decisions in the life of political activism with frankness about something liberation movements prefer to keep to themselves. Other political prisoners were offered conditional release at the same time, and some took it. 'Suddenly there was the possibility of being released and each of us who rejected the offer had to fight the temptation to accept it. Precisely because we had to fight so hard, we could not allow ourselves to sympathise with our comrades who had accepted the offer.'

This is confessed not to assert exceptional bravery and fortitude; it emerges in self-reproach, as witness of his own behaviour—in retrospect he finds bitter rejection of other comrades reprehensible and has sought to heal the break now that all are out of prison.

❧

Within Niehaus there are many examples to learn of the Cain-and-Abel situation that existed in our country for so long. It was the essential form of communication, dire, of our time, between family and rebel of conscience, between the authority of the state and the authority of virtue; between the law of respect for human life and the perceived necessity of violence to gain that respect for all.

Niehaus did not cause anyone's death, but both he and Kasrils did accept the philosophy and practice of a just war, which, plainly expressed, proposes justified deaths, whether performed by one's own hand or that of someone else. In their testimony we learn much of the nature of the society, our Age of Apartheid, which created these men in answer to a terrible, apocalyptic need. In another time, in a social order without a long history of systematic State violence, without that need for revolt, what might these men have been? Kasrils perhaps a theatre entrepreneur, a television personality; Niehaus a minister of religion. It is unlikely either would have written a book. That they have done so bears witness to events that were half-told and situations, moral choices that were half-known, providing valuable documentation of the past we have just emerged from.

❧

'We make of the quarrel with others, rhetoric; but of our quarrel with ourselves, poetry,' writes Yeats.

Beneath the rhetoric of the political struggle, which is inseparable from testimony, we have seen that there may be, also, the quarrel with oneself.

It is poets who can internalize the quarrel with others—the political struggle—within the quarrel with themselves: the question of being.

Jeremy Cronin, white, son of an officer in the South African Navy, was a young university lecturer in philosophy and politics when he became a revolutionary and a member of Umkhonto we Sizwe, making pamphlet bombs that sowed opposition to the white minority government in the stony streets of apartheid. On trial under the Terrorism Act, he too, like Niehaus, refused to plead guilty. He told the court he believed what he had done was right; he would do it again. Later, he was to reflect in a poem:

> I think of what Engels said
> about freedom being
> the understanding of necessity.

For in prison, on scraps of paper, on sheets slipped between study assignments by correspondence, he wrote poetry. One of his poems creates a photograph, never taken, in which he groups himself with other prisoners of conscience, his jail comrades.

> There we are, seven of us
> (but why the grinning?)
> Seven of us, seated in a circle,
> The unoccupied place in the centre stands for what
>   happened
> Way outside the frame of this photo.

He is referring to the scene of actions they took together before being imprisoned, but the poetry in his book, entitled *Inside,* stands for and is a revelation of what happens within him and within others in prison, way outside the frame of any fixed images. Prison alone is the frame. The unoccupied place in the centre is the space that is filled by the poet's transformation of

the experience of prison, an opening-out of a sealed compart-
ment of life where the mind, the emotions, the spirit interact
intensely in a painfully inescapable process of self-knowledge.

How much better this is expressed in his own brief distilla-
tion: 'you commune with the stale bread of yourself.'

Prison diet as a metaphor for the bread of life, the spiritual
hunger of a man in solitary confinement: the abstract bread-of-
life concept is broken apart to release new meaning, becomes
a poignant paradox. To break bread is to share it, commune
with another; in solitary confinement there is only the self.

Where testimony gives account of family ties and conflict in
narrative, the poet Cronin sums up his childhood of conflict in
a conventional white-supremacist background with perfect totality as 'this thing stuck to my feet.' In this tactile image each
of us at once recognizes that shadow of self which is attached
to one's passage forever. And a metaphor for the liberation of
prisoners becomes that of the liberation of the people of South
Africa when the poet fashions a bird out of a pair of socks, a
playing card, and scraps from the prison workshop, and releases
it to the world:

> I check your hungry parts
> over again, longing by longing then
> out
> over the high walls I launch you now . . .

And the bird he has made is a shrike, a bird of prey; there
is challenge, a defiance as well as longing for freedom, in the
launching: the message to 'outside' from 'inside' is that injustice
is still and always shall be under attack.

Mongane Wally Serote comes from the black ghettoes, a
poet who has lived through solitary confinement without trial

and many years of exile. He has side-stepped death in Africa and while followed by assassins in the streets of London. His revolutionary activity and his poetry are conditional for existence each upon the other as flesh is to blood. His long poems are an inner discourse that flows through the definitive experience of our country in the immediate past and the transitional present. In *A Tough Tale,* written while exiled, he writes as a black, but in *Third World Express,* written since his return home to South Africa, he writes as a man to whom the co-existence of human beings is the ultimate identity; he speaks of and for black and white.

In the earlier book he conveys the suffering of black people with a vivid passion that follows one's eyes whenever one turns away—carrying Yeats's 'terrible beauty', Serote's tale is a classic of human pain extracted from lifetimes of actuality:

> There is no way this tale can be told
> by a little man like me
> it is a tale
> fresh every minute and every hour
> it is a gurgle tale of blood
> a fugue
> it is a tale of deaths died in strange ways and places
> . . .
> it is told by running footsteps at night
> this tale
> is told in the streets of my town
> in the alleys of the night hour
> it is told by the surge of masses of people.

In place of describing oppressive laws he creates a litany of those who live under them:

38

We
We are men and women, children
. . .
We sleep with our boots on.

In the later book, *Third World Express,* the man-hunting grounds, the fear-filled black ghettoes, a life utterly without privacy from police informers is conveyed by mutterings

so-and-so is pissing
so-and-so is shitting
so-and-so is sleeping with so-and-so
so-and-so didn't shit or piss today
so-and-so says the hunting grounds are quiet,
so-and-so says there's noise in the hunting grounds.

For, the poet says

We want the world to know:
we have come a long way now
we are not like spotless white shirts
we are khaki
it is the time, the road, the dust, the heat, the rain and the
    wind
which did it all.

In imagery weathered with suffering, setting the commonplace deliberately jarring against the eternals, he fulfils an admonition of his own:

In the heart of this time
it is the simple things which are forgotten
desecrated
and defiled
they are fossilized into a past which is out of reach.

39

This past stands for the denial of the lives of black people by whites; the long discounting of their existence as feeling and thinking humans. It is a past that extends naturally from his people to that of the poor and preyed-upon of the world, in a vision of migratory birds:

> despair, with which the spirit of ghosts
> still sings on rows of telephone wires
> where birds sing in chorus with bundles of resting souls
> with heaps of life lost
> in the insatiable fathom of civilisation
> for what
> Africa
> Asia
> Latin America, for what?

Serote is a strict moralist in the context of the kind of South Africa he has found on his return. It takes courage—outgrowth of a base of virtue that is belief beyond discrimination in both the worth and the fallibility of human beings—for a black revolutionary to accuse other blacks. In his task to press truth from the contradictions within himself and his society he speaks of men and women

> blacks and whites who have left droplets of blood on my
>   shoes
> these droplets don't ever dry up
> in a place
> on a train
> in a bus
> in different cities
> I see the droplets on my shoes
> *me*

❦

```
I
will not hide them
I walk
I fly I ride I cycle
in big and small cities
me
I can't forget
I don't understand
the droplets are still fresh and wet on my shoes.
```

He will not betray by any denial of their existence those drops of blood drawn by the wounds of the past, but the poetry of his return home is informed with a love of life; he yearns for healing, not revenge.

```
What can we do
for
this world, which we share and shape
whose corners you can touch if you stretch your arms
whose roof you can reach if you stand up
was and is ours
we make and have made it
because
all of us die from what we all have eaten and have done.
```

The ethos of Serote's and Cronin's poetry is *restoration:* of the spirit beyond and above setting the story straight, which is the business and usefulness of testimony.

The imagination has a longer reach. And in more senses than one. When testimony has been filed, out of date, poetry continues to carry the experience from which the narrative has fallen away. It is in the lines of Homer that the Greek experience definitive for humankind lives on among us. From the poets comes what Octavio Paz terms our 'metahistory . . . a common end that lay above individuals and had to do with values that were . . . transcendent.'

But for the present, in which we in South Africa are attempting to reconstruct our country and our lives in unfamiliar freedom, learning the dangers that, like responsibility, come with freedom, both the testimony and the literature are vital. We are that determined people Serote writes of, on that morning Serote predicted:

> One morning
> my people will hang on a sunrise . . . we shall stand face to
>   face with the sun . . . leaving behind us
> so many dead
> wounded
> mad
> so many senseless things
> we shall have buried apartheid—how shall we shake hands
> how shall we hug each other that day? . . . What first words
>   will we utter?

We are searching for those words. Wounded, precarious; yet hanging on a sunrise.

3

ZAABALAWI: THE CONCEALED SIDE
The Cairo Trilogy

NAGUIB MAHFOUZ

Naguib Mahfouz, Chinua Achebe, Amos Oz: the Arab, the African, the Jew. Do I group these writers together because of the racial and political typology their ethnic identity could represent, criss-crossing the Arab-Israeli conflict and the conflict between white and black, for which the African-as-black and the Jew-as-white could stand?

The oppositional links are there, of course, as the obvious. But these three writers do not expound the obvious; divided by race, country and religion, they enter by their separate ways territory unknown, in a common pursuit that doesn't have to be acknowledged in any treaty: is simply there.

Proust wrote: 'Do not be afraid to go too far, for the truth lies beyond.' These are writers at one in being ready to go too far.

Too far for the accepted norms of loyalty to the regimes, the societies, the mores, the politics of the countries whose earth, nevertheless, they feel between bare toes, flesh of the flesh.

Mahfouz was banned, years ago, from publishing one of his early novels in Egypt, more recently placed under the edict of a *fatwa* for blasphemy in his writings, and in 1994 stabbed, badly injured, by a religious extremist while on his way to a weekly meeting in a Cairo café with fellow writers. Amos Oz was regarded as a traitor Arab-lover in some circles in Israel until 'Peace Now' became the accepted political ethic in 1994, and was again regarded as a traitor by Israelis opposed to the various Israeli-Arab peace initiatives and agreements that followed. Chinua Achebe was forced into exile over his writings and actions in support of Biafra during the Nigerian civil war.

One of these writers, Naguib Mahfouz, wrote a parable in which a sick man goes on a pilgrimage through all quarters of the ancient city of Cairo to find the saintly shaykh, Zaabalawi, to heal him. Everybody he asks for directions sends him somewhere different.

'God be with you,' says one. 'For who knows, O Zaabalawi, where you are?'

'Do those who need him suffer as I do?' the sick man asks.

And the reply comes: 'Such suffering is part of the cure.'

Told at last he will find Zaabalawi in one of the saintly dissolute's regular haunts, a bar, the weary man falls asleep waiting for him to appear. When he awakes, he finds his head is wet. The others in the bar tell him that Zaabalawi came while he was asleep, and sprinkled water on him to refresh him. Having had this sign of Zaabalawi's existence, the sick soul will go on searching for him all his life—*'Yes I have to find Zaabalawi.'*

The search for truth is a cliché of literary purpose; is it not what all literature is about, for only the truth, if we could find it, makes sense of life?

But the truth has another meaning, and one that is sought by these three writers out of the dangerous contradictions of their particular societies.

The truth is the real definition of 'home': it is the final destination of the human spirit beyond national boundaries, natal traditions. These writers know *who* they are, their work is no part of the Euro-American search for identity; what it expresses is the sense that it is not that the individual does not know himself, it is that as Amos Oz's character Fima says, *'his place does not know him.'*

In Israel, in Egypt, in Nigeria, the real Home to be attained is, in Oz's quote from the Aramaic, *sitra de-itkasia:* The Concealed Side.

These novels are works that go too far, they're after Zaabalawi, looking for that Home on The Concealed Side.

The three writers have another difference from most writers who share the pursuit of truth in its elusive guises. They do not belong to the main stream of Euro-American literature.

Despite their brilliance—and all three are outstanding in contemporary literature—despite the fact that Mahfouz is a Nobel Laureate, Achebe's work is studied in universities all over the world, Oz's work is read in twenty-six languages, they are not much quoted by literary scholars outside the classroom and Ph.D. theses, seldom cited as among the most important writers of our time, have not given rise to the imitation by lesser writers that seems to be the accepted mark of fame and worth in Western literary canons.

They present the other world: for Mahfouz and Achebe, the post-colonial world that bears on the face of ancient Egypt and old Africa the paint and patches of foreign occupations; for Oz, the opposite existential mode, the reoccupation of an ancient

45

territory by an ancient people's (contested) right that creates colonial power over other ancient inhabitants.

Yet despite these writers' differences from what might be called the main stream of literature, their work arches across the poles apart characteristic of our time: the age of commitment, and the age of alienation, by which our century surely shall be known. These writers are engaged in this war within us: the fanaticism which can arise from the nobility of the one, the deathly apathy which can arise from the other.

Naguib Mahfouz's *Cairo Trilogy* is a mighty pyramid of creativity, if I may invoke an image from the country out of which it is made.

The three volumes, *Palace Walk, Palace of Desire* and *Sugar Street,* encompass the years from 1918, the end of one war, to 1944, the last months of another. The three addresses are at once the houses where the members of al-Sayid Ahmad Abd al-Jawad's family and their collaterals live at different periods; the personification of different levels of society in Cairo; and the different political and moral values and sexual mores enacted within their walls. Standing while all else rises and falls, the houses also represent the final authority, the power of time, which contains all.

Al-Sayid Ahmad Abd al-Jawad is the pivot on which the life of the Palace Walk house turns. He is a paradigm of sensuality as authority, one of those beings in whom paradox of characteristics, at once awful and beguiling, is life-force. He prays 'with the same enthusiasm he invested in every aspect of life, pouring himself into each. When he worked, he put his whole heart into it. If he befriended someone, he was exceptionally affectionate . . . He did not drink without getting drunk . . . He was earnest and sincere in everything. His life was com-

posed of a diversity of mutually contradictory elements, waver-
ing between piety and depravity.'

This earnestness and sincerity extend to his tyranny over his
wife, Amina; his sons, Yasin, Fahmy and Kamal; and his daughters, Khadija and Aisha. The atmosphere of his house, where
everyone assembles for Amina's coffee-hour, 'he strove to keep
one of stern purity and immaculate innocence'—and this while
he is out every night drinking with his friends, making music,
and making love to a series of prostitutes.

Like a Choderlos de Laclos or a Kawabata, Mahfouz is able
with a touch of coarseness to create eroticism without scenes
of sexual gyration. The style of Jawad's sexual life is set here
and there in a line or two, as when one of his discarded
mistresses, engaged as a singer at his daughter's wedding, says
to the male guests gathered in a room apart, 'Gentlemen, you're
my witnesses. Observe how this man, who used to be unhappy
if he couldn't stick the tip of his mustache in my belly button,
can't bear the sight of me.'

In the trilogy the remarkable exploration of the patterns of
sexuality—the sexual politics contained within the politics of
traditional societies—the will to power, the absurdities and
beauties, the final betrayal of self, begins with Jawad.

> Despite his number of amorous adventures . . . al-Sayid Ahmad
> had experienced only lust . . . He had elevated lust to its most
> exalted type . . . his conjugal love was affected by calm elements
> of affection and familiarity, but in essence it continued to be
> based on bodily desire. When an emotion is of this type . . . it
> cannot be content with only one form of expression. Thus he
> had shot off in pursuit of all the varieties of love and passion,
> like a wild bull. No woman was anything more than a body to
> him. All the same he would not bow his head before that body

unless he found it truly worthy of being seen, touched, smelled, tasted, and heard. It was lust, yes, but not bestial or blind. It had been refined by a craft that was humour, and good cheer.

The failure of this sophisticated sexual aestheticism, itself a tyranny mirroring Jawad's own kind towards his family, Mahfouz establishes as the *paradox of excess as unfulfilment*—Jawad's 'thirst for love.'

Jawad is unable, by his egoism, and by his tendency to flout all religious taboos away from Palace Walk and to impose religious orthodoxy with exaggerated strictness within its walls, to slake that thirst among his family. Love is exacted from his wife, Amina, in the form of worshipful fear. Craven, she supports him in his edict that the daughters may not be seen by any prospective suitor and are to marry only according to the father's choice. And she accepts that she herself may never leave the house, Palace Walk, unless escorted by her jailor husband to visit her mother.

His eldest son by his first marriage, Yasin, seethes with unexpressed rebellion against the father from whom he has inherited sensuality without Jawad's strength of character. Fahmy, the contemplative law student, loves and is adored by his mother, and Kamal is a child who is as yet innocent, taking his father's strictness as a protection within which he pursues a cosy happiness in the love of his brothers and sisters.

In the only interview with Mahfouz I have ever been able to find—he rightly prefers his work to speak for him—he was asked: 'What is the subject closest to your heart?' And he replied, 'Freedom. Freedom from colonization, freedom from the absolute rule of kings, and basic human freedom in the context of society and the family. These types of freedom follow from one to the other. In the trilogy, for example, after the revolution brought political freedom, Abdul Jawad's family demanded more freedom from *him*.'

The first attempt at the types of freedom that flow one from the other comes in *Palace Walk,* a note sounding in anticipation and warning of the trumpet flourishes of family rebellion that will sound in *Palace of Desire* and culminate along with political change in *Sugar Street.* An act against the authority of the father prefigures acts against the political regime, with which such domestic acts will be inextricably bound.

Jawad goes on a business trip to Port Said. Yasin suggests to his mother, Amina: 'Why don't you have some fun, too? . . . Nobody lives like us.'

Amina has never seen the district in which she has lived for forty years. She is persuaded to go out secretly, with the child Kamal, to fulfil the dream of her life and visit the al-Husayn Mosque. On the way home she is struck by a car and her shoulder-bone is fractured. Jawad thus discovers her deceit and disobedience. When she recovers, he casts her out of the house. She goes to her mother, disgraced and heart-broken rather than resentful: her husband has exerted his right.

What subtlety Mahfouz achieves here, as often, by changing focus from protagonists to someone the reader has barely noticed! The charged emotions when Amina's sons, Yasin, Fahmy and Kamal, come to see her are suddenly conveyed through a dimension of comprehension that cannot be theirs, it is that of the old blind woman, Amina's mother.

A minor character; yes, but there are few such extras dismissed, never to be on call again, in the richly-peopled three-volume work. What appear to be closed encounters reopen, recur, in subsequent contexts which slowly yield their originally unrecognized portent and meaning.

Never are these convenient authorial coincidences. It is that Jawad's family, like ourselves with only our five senses, do not recognize the signs that are given; one of the obstacles in the way of reaching The Concealed Side. The officer who exchanged lovers' signals with the beautiful younger daughter, Aisha, through the slats of the screened balcony at Palace Walk, and whom, consequently, she was forbidden to marry, seems long forgotten when she has been married off to a son of the prominent Shawkat family of Sugar Street, lived a doll's life of pretty clothes and sweetmeats, been widowed and bereft of her children. Years later, at Sugar Street, the officer comes to arrest her sister's sons during the uprisings against King Faruk. Aisha does not recognize him or his name. More than a loss of memory; hers is the alienated state of having turned away from, missed out on, the path of genuine feelings which was offered her, and whose significance for her life was unrecognized.

Political attitudes in the family are dominated throughout the trilogy by resentment against the British occupation of Egypt.

In the years of *Palace Walk,* Jawad wants the caliphate claimed by the Ottoman sultans to regain power and exiled Khedive Abbas II to return, and says of the Australian troops who during the 1914–18 war have made the Ezbekiya district of his nightly pleasures out of bounds: 'May God destroy and annihilate them.'

Youthful Yasin and Fahmy, during the Second World War, want the Germans to win, although Yasin asks: 'But what will you say if we discover the Germans are just the way the English describe them?'

As the 1914–18 war ends, the Wafd, which originally simply meant 'delegation', and presented to the British High Commis-

sioner the case for Egypt's independence, is formed as a political
party. Even conservative Jawad signs the petition to authorize
the nationalist leaders to proceed to Britain, although his political fervour is expressed inevitably in terms of his more
dominant passion: 'I'm so happy about this petition that I could
be a drunkard lifting his eighth glass between Zubayda's thighs.'

But revolutionary politics is no longer merely one of the
subjects of discussion among male companions in coffee houses
and at drinking parties, the traditional life ordered by religion
and authoritarianism. It enters the house.

Fahmy joins a student activist group when martial law is
declared in Cairo after the Wafd under Sa'd Zaghlul has been
prevented from going to present the petition in London. Secretly, Fahmy distributes banned pamphlets and takes part in
protest meetings. 'He could not have stood for life to have
continued in its calm deliberate way, treading beneath it the
destinies and hopes of men.'

As a result, Jawad is plunged into the crisis over commitment
that must come to all traditionalist liberals in revolutionary
situations. His son 'a friend of the freedom fighters . . . had the
flood reached his roost? . . . He had nothing against the freedom fighters . . . he prayed for their success as the conclusion
of his normal prayers. News about the strike, acts of sabotage,
and the battles had filled him with hope and admiration, but it
was a totally different matter for any of these deeds to be
performed by a son of his. His children were meant to be a
breed apart, outside the framework of history. He alone would
see the course for them, not the revolution, the times, or the
rest of humanity.'

The father demands that Fahmy swear he will 'break every
link' between himself and the revolution. In a scene of terrifying
power Jawad's brutal eloquence threatens: 'Don't mistake me

for some old woman. You sons of bitches are driving me crazy
. . . I'm going to hand you over to the police myself . . . myself,
you son of a bitch. The only word that counts here is mine.
Mine, mine, mine . . . Did you think you were a man? If I
wanted, I'd beat you till your skull caved in.'

But it is the new power, the power of the revolution, and
not the old power of patriarchal wrath that destroys the boy.

When Sa'd Zaghlul is released from detention Fahmy joins
a celebratory demonstration for which official permission has
been given. At the Ezbekiya Garden, soldiers are gathered and
in treachery fire into the demonstrators. Fahmy is killed.

The news reaches the father in his shop. The devastating
restraint with which Mahfouz sounds the clash of sorrow against
the continuity of commonplace comes when Jawad returns to
the house in Palace Walk. As he enters he hears his youngest
son, Kamal, singing a song we can guess must be familiar to
Jawad from his carousing nights with the singers Jalila and
Zubayda:

> Visit me once each year
> for it's wrong to abandon people forever.

Kamal, singing the continuity of life on the last page of *Palace
Walk,* the charming child in whose innocent affection the
frustrations of his sisters, the smouldering rebellion of his brothers, and the oppression of his mother are all dissolved, now
displaces al-Sayid Ahmad Abd al-Jawad as the centre of
Mahfouz's contemplation in the second volume, *Palace of Desire.*

I use the term 'contemplation' rather than 'attention' because
Mahfouz has the gift of only great writers to contemplate all

the possibilities inherent in his characters rather than discard this and that awkwardness for consistency. So much that is beyond comprehension in human behaviour, let alone rationalisation; yet literature is, by its very ordering into words, grammar, a rationalisation; Mahfouz struggles with this, resists as far as any single agent of creativity can, leaving us with the complex honesty of aspects for which a final containing design cannot be given: it belongs to The Concealed Side. Searching for it, he is not afraid of rousing repugnance for a personage or an act on one page, and affection, even admiration for the one or empathy with the other, on the next page. The stimulus of his writings comes from the conflict of responses he elicits.

Palace of Desire is not just a new location into which a member of the family—Yasin—moves to get away from his father's disapproval of his divorce; it is the realm of sensuality which reigns in this second part of the trilogy counterpoint to that other human drive, freedom conceived of as attainable in political struggle.

In societies where domination by an outside power exists or has existed, the *occupation of the national personality* is resisted not by obvious means alone—political opposition and rebellion, religious fervour, cultural assertion—but also, perhaps, by the display of sexual energy as a force that has not been, cannot be, touched by alien authority: the life-force itself.

Al-Sayid Ahmad Abd al-Jawad, feeling alienated by the revolution after it has killed Fahmy, has gradually 'returned to his original pro-nationalist feelings because of the respect and esteem people showered on him as the father of a martyr.' (Mahfouz's wry indication of how the vanity of self-image in Jawad's personality is able to overcome grief.)

At the same time, Jawad's form of mourning by giving up

his mistresses comes to an end. Encouraged by his male coterie, he returns to a houseboat on the Nile and becomes the slavish sugar-daddy of Zanuba the lute player, who, unknown to either father or son, also goes drunk to bed with Yasin, the sensual appetites of father and son making this inevitable rather than coincidental.

'Desire was a blind and merciless tyrant.' A tyrant over the tyrant father, the discovery of which, some time before, when Yasin in a brothel secretly watched his father carousing with one of his old mistresses, has ended the bane of and also the only discipline in Yasin's hedonistic life: his awe of parental authority.

Seventeen-year-old Kamal knows nothing of the women his father rejoices in as 'each massively beautiful as the ceremonial camel when it sets off for Mecca with the pilgrims.' But his extreme sensibility picks up the aura of sensuality emanating from his beloved father and the clownish sexual exploits of his brother Yasin, who, when Kamal was a child, had flung himself upon the elderly respectable family servant. This aura possibly is responsible for the revulsion against sex, the torture of its separation, in his emotions, from love, that is to distort Kamal's entire life. He feels: 'I instinctively hate man's animal nature from the depths of my heart.'

In the creation of Kamal, Mahfouz does not only produce a Kafkian fictional personality (see "Wedding Preparations in the Country" and "The Judgment"); here rather is Kafka himself, recording the repulsion roused in him at the sight of his parents' night-clothes on their bed. Kamal is idealistically, passionately in love with Aïda Shaddad, sister of his closest school friend, but the thought of marriage with her revolts him. While enchanted by Aïda's beauty he rejects any notion of her body's sexual function. At a family gathering he reflects 'These people

are talking about beauty. What do they know about its essence
. . . If you ask me about beauty I won't speak of a pure bronze
complexion, tranquil black eyes, a slim figure, and Parisian
elegance . . . Beauty itself is a painful convulsion of the heart,
an abundance of vitality in the soul, and a mad chase under-
taken by the spirit until it encounters the heavens.'

Only vaguely understood by him is his other revulsion with
which the first is linked, and which is also to influence his life
profoundly: a revulsion against bourgeois materialism, values
and class prejudice in a society where matings are arranged to
consolidate alliances of wealth and prestige between families of
young people who have never seen one another until the
wedding day, let alone fallen in love.

'It is marriage itself,' Kamal says, 'that seems to bring love
down from its heaven to the earth of contractual relationships
and sweaty exertion.' The concatenation of property and sex.
Against this is the beginning of Kamal's inner revolution while
the nationalist leader Sa'd Zaghlul is setting off for Europe to
pursue Egypt's political revolution in demands for the independence which still, long after the declaration of 1922, has not
been achieved.

Contrary to his father's will and as the object of his father's
scorn, Kamal refuses to study law as the opening to a prestigious
future in government service. He opts for what he sees as
knowledge for himself and others for its own sake: what is
regarded as the lowly occupation of teacher.

It is not enthusiasm for pedagogy that decides him, but
bewilderment. Rejecting the values of Palace Walk as home,
while still physically part of the family coffee-hour, he makes
the first move through personal integrity towards the Home
that is truth.

Another house—the house, the district where Kamal pursues

his love for Aïda—exemplifies the paradoxes in which he places himself while still young.

The Shaddad mansion in the smart district of al-Abbasiya is that of the *haute bourgeoisie,* a Europeanised family who have lived in Paris and whose women appear in public—a setting, ironically, far more materialistic, if freer, than Palace Walk. And it is here that he is sometimes even able to talk to the girl he worships while rejecting the sexual source of the attraction. Haughty, skilled in the tease of disdain, she gives him some ambiguous signs of hope that she might be attracted to him but all the time is promised to another of the circle of young men who gather to talk politics in the Shaddad garden, iconoclastic in what Aïda's brother, Husayn, calls 'A nation whose most notable manifestations are tombs and corpses.'

Kamal finds that

> Strangely enough the political activities of the day present an enlarged version of his life. When he read about developments in the newspapers [in the hostility against the English occupation a titled British official has been murdered, with consequent restrictive reprisals] he could have been reading about the events at Palace Walk. Like Kamal, Sa'd Zaghlul was as good as imprisoned and the victim of . . . treacherous betrayal . . . They had suffered because of contacts with people distinguished both by the loftiness of their aristocratic backgrounds and by the baseness of their deeds. The personal distress of the great nationalist leader also resembled the vanquished state of the nation. Kamal felt the same emotion and passion about the political situation as he did about his personal condition.

The pull between the personal and the historico-political is manifest in all the residents of Palace Walk.

The revolution undermines the traditional authority of the old domestic regime as well as that of the old political regime, so that Amina is now free to go about and visit her beloved al-Husayn Mosque.

Kamal remarks to his mother: 'You're not a prisoner in the house as you once were . . . Imagine what you would have missed if father had not relaxed the rules.' But Amina's answer is: 'I wish I had remained as I was and kept my son.'

The old guard represented at Palace Walk gives up no more easily than British imperial power, however. Kamal in his loss of faith along with loss of love—'Where's religion? It's gone! I've lost it . . . and I've lost Aïda and my self-confidence too'—writes an article expounding Darwinism. Hardly daring for the West in the late Twenties, but in orthodox Islam a heresy. His father fulminates: 'Couldn't you find some other subject besides this criminal theory to write about?'

Kamal in his search for The Concealed Side has turned desperately from readings of the great poets and sceptics of Islam, Abu al-A la al-Ma'arri and Umar al-Khayyam, to readings in the materialist philosophy of the West.

He questions himself: 'Why had he written this article? . . . He must have wanted to announce the demise of his religious belief . . . Science's iron fist had destroyed it once and for all.'

Kamal has often dreamt of writing what he thinks of as an 'all-inclusive book' containing the essence of faith and philosophy, all the knowledge mankind needs to live by, although, while he was still a Believer this was hubris in view of the existence of the book-of-books, the Qur'an.

But now: 'What was left of the original subject matter? He no longer considered the prophets to have been prophets, Heaven and Hell did not exist. The study of man was merely a branch of animal science . . . Yet his idealism refuses to be put out by the light of science . . . There is a struggle towards truth aiming at the good of mankind as a whole. In my opinion, life would be meaningless without that.'

His friend Husayn defines Kamal's kind of faith: 'The Believer derives his love for these values from religion, while the free man loves them for themselves.'

But a coalition of Sa'd Zaghlul with his former traitors as political expediency in the revolution sours the consolation with political disillusion. Again Kamal asks himself: 'Is there anything in this world that has lived up to your hopes?'

He turns aside, as many seekers after truth have before him, to alcohol, which he never has tasted. If, in the low-life bars of Cairo, he does not happen upon the one that Zaabalawi frequents, with his first whisky binge he enters a state which creates a meditation on the effects of alcohol unsurpassed in originality by anything I have read.

A discharge of psychic heat raced off through his veins. The sorrow sealing his soul's vessel dissolved. I've felt something like this . . . before . . . Oh, what a memory . . . it was love! The day she [Aïda] called out 'Kamal,' that intoxicated you before you knew what intoxication was . . . Admit your long history with inebriation. You've been rowdy for ages, travelling passion's drunken path . . . Alcohol's the spirit of love once love's inner lining of pain is stripped away . . . This captivating intoxication is the secret of life and its ultimate goal. Alcohol's only the precursor and the symbol for it . . . wine's a necessary scout for human happiness. The question boils down to this: How can we turn life into a perpetual state of intoxication without resort to alcohol? We won't find the answer through debate, productivity, fighting, or exertion. All those are means to an end, not ends in themselves.

Kamal seems to believe he has encountered Zaabalawi in that bar where the sick man missed him; he has his revelation of The Concealed Side, even if it resembles Nirvana strangely arrived at: 'Happiness will never be realised until we free ourselves from the exploitation of any means whatsoever. Then we can live a purely intellectual and spiritual life untainted by anything. This is the happiness for which alcohol proves a representation.'

It is also the creed of evasion, this vision let out of the whisky bottle. Sobered, Kamal cannot follow it.

He tells himself, 'The problem's not that truth is harsh but that liberation from ignorance is as painful as being born. Run after truth until you're breathless.'

The wild race includes forcing himself to end his ignorance of carnal experience. This brother who seeks the freedom of virtue meets his dissolute elder brother in a brothel; and Yasin in ribald courteous welcome offers Kamal first turn with the chosen woman.

Alone with her, Kamal cannot perform. Sex immediately reminds him of the violation of Aïda's body by another man, her husband, its invasion by pregnancy. His revulsion, mixed with the urges he eventually comes to satisfy regularly with the prostitute, is as pitiful as that Althusser recounts as a source of the insanity that led to him killing his wife. Kamal says to Yasin: 'Man's a filthy creature. Couldn't he have been created better and cleaner?'

And Yasin says: 'Man's a filthy creature? Were you offended by my comments on women? The fact is that I love them. I love them with all their faults. But I wanted to demonstrate that the angelic woman does not exist. In fact, if she did, I doubt I'd love her. Like your father, I love full hips. An angel with a heavy bottom wouldn't be able to fly.' Spirit and flesh constantly alternate in the seat of power, in life; Yasin is life's principle, for the moment, here.

Kamal, seeing himself as purely the result of materialist causes, 'nothing but a drop of sperm ejected because of an innocent desire for pleasure, a pressing need for solace . . . or even a feeling of obligation towards a wife confined to the house', comes home drunk that night and composes a letter to his begetter comparable only to Kafka's letter to *his* father, and, like Kafka's letter, never to be delivered.

Father, let me tell you what's on my mind. I'm not angry about what I've learned about your character, because I like the newly discovered side better than the familiar one. I admire your charm, grace, impudence, rowdiness and adventuresome spirit . . . the side all your acquaintances love . . . But I'd like to ask why you choose to show us this frightening and gruff mask? . . . We've known you as a tyrannical despot. All the same I still love and admire you, even if the godlike qualities my enchanted eyes once associated with you have faded away. Yes, your power lives on only as a legend . . . But you're not the only one whose image has changed. God Himself's no longer the god I used to worship. I'm sifting His essential attributes to rid them of tyranny, despotism, dictatorship, compulsion, and similar human traits . . . My soul tells me I'll never stop and that debate, no matter how painful, is better than resignation and slumber . . . Do you know the consequences there were to loving you despite your tyranny? I loved another tyrant . . . she oppressed me without ever loving me . . . Father, you're the one who made it easy for me to accept oppression through your continual tyranny. And you, Mother . . . ignorance is your crime, ignorance . . . My father's the manifestation of ignorant harshness and you of ignorant tenderness. As long as I live I'll remain the victim of these two opposites. It's your ignorance,

❦

too, that filled my spirit with legends. You're my link to the Stone Age. How miserable I am now as I try to liberate myself from your influence. And I'll be just as miserable in the future when I free myself from my father. For this reason, I propose . . . that the family be abolished . . . Indeed, grant me a nation with no history and a life without a past.

Palace of Desire closes with the arrival of Kamal through his rites of passage at a lonely inner place outside the mosque, outside the family mores, where only 'In the distance, visible through a telescope, was the mountain of reality on which was inscribed its password: Open your eyes and be courageous.' Egypt's hero of the exile, the revolution, the liberation and the constitution has died. Kamal mourns Sa'd Zaghlul, admiring him as much as his heroes Copernicus, the chemist Ostwald, or the physicist Mach: he says: 'for an effort to link Egypt with the advance of human progress is noble and human. Patriotism's a virtue if it's not tainted by xenophobia. Of course, hating England is a form of self-defense.'

In the context of an occupied country, in place of being chauvinist, that kind of nationalism becomes, as he puts it, 'nothing more than a local manifestation of a concern for human rights.'

❦

Sugar Street is the cartographical signifier under which the surge of life takes up the next generation.

Sugar Street, the final volume of the trilogy, begins roughly ten years after the end of *Palace of Desire* and after fifty-four years of British occupation of Egypt. At Palace Walk Kamal is 'sad to watch the family age . . . his father, who had been so forceful and mighty grow weak . . . his mother wasting away and disappearing into old age', the disintegration into an almost catatonic state of that once charming caged butterfly, his sister Aisha.

For—again like Franz Kafka himself rather than a Kafkian character—Kamal, who has savagely proposed that the family be abolished, cannot summon the will to leave Palace Walk. A divided self cannot act: he spends half his time teaching and studying philosophy, and the opposing half

> in satisfying various needs . . . of the animal concealed inside him. That creature's goals were limited to self-preservation and the gratification of desires . . . He escaped his loneliness by adopting Spinoza's notion of the unity of existence and consoled himself for his humiliations by participating in Schopenhauer's ascetic victory over desire . . . Yet this continuous effort did not succeed in disarming the anxiety that tormented him, for truth was a beloved as flirtatious, inaccessible, and coquettish as any human sweetheart . . . awakening a violent desire to possess it and to merge with it.

Release from warring self-absorption comes through occasional identification with the ordinary people around him. Though he seems never to belong among them,

> His heart could not ignore the life of the Egyptian people. It was aroused by anything affecting them . . . While his intellect was temporarily sealed up as if in a bottle, psychic forces ordinarily suppressed burst forth, eager for an existence filled with emotions and sensations . . . his life was revitalized . . . his loneliness melted away . . . For the time being he would postpone consideration of the problems of matter, spirit, physics or metaphysics, in order to concentrate on what these people loved and hated . . . the constitution, the economic crisis, the political

situation and the nationalist cause . . . He needs an hour when he can escape through the embrace of society from the vexations of his life.

But 'it would have been unnatural for him to adopt this life permanently.'

The embrace of society without commitment to which, in certain countries in certain eras, one becomes the 'superfluous man' first encountered in nineteenth-century literature—this embrace of society belongs to the new generation of Jawad's family.

Sugar Street is where Khadija, Kamal's domineering elder sister, married, like Aisha, into the house of the Shawkat family. There, her sons Abd al-Muni'm and Ahmad take up that embrace of commitment. Abd al-Muni'm is a member of the Muslim Brotherhood; Ahmad is a Communist.

Abd al-Muni'm proselytizes: 'We attempt to understand Islam as God intended it to be: a religion, a way of life, a code of law, and a political system . . . Let us prepare for a prolonged struggle. Our mission is not to Egypt alone but to all Muslims world-wide . . . We shall not put our weapons away until the Qur'an has become a constitution for all Believers.'

He is asked by a fellow student: 'Is talk like this appropriate for the twentieth century?'

His reply is ominous when read by us towards the end of that century: he says: 'and for the hundred and twentieth century, too.'

'Do you stone people who disagree with you?' the student challenges.

And we answer, yes, and you pronounce the *fatwa* of death on writers, too. Mahfouz, way back in 1957, when he published this volume set in the Thirties, understood his world well

enough to foreshadow the Muslim fundamentalism that would
distort a great religion into a threat against hope of democracy
not only in Egypt but in many other countries of the world,
and thrust a knife into his neck.

Ahmad's turn to Communism is the natural phenomenon of
youth in countries that have lived under the imperialist rule of
the West and the pashas of indigenous tradition who have
colluded with it. Marx and Lenin offer, as no other ideology
does, the iconoclastic right and will-power to plough down
palaces. Even today, when the founding experiments of Communism have failed terribly, the phenomenon continues to
occur, because the theory authorizes that right and will-power,
just as the teachings of Christ authorize the right of and will
towards good, although horrors have been perpetrated in the
name of Christianity, most recently under apartheid in South
Africa. Abd al-Muni'm and Ahmad are the children of a social
and political revolution: the cleared ground is bewildering;
choices of new structures to live by must be made, and democracy offers the least immediate, emotionally appealing, fix.
Their situation prefigures what has been repeated in many
countries of the continent of Africa to which Egypt belongs.

In this work that moves majestically in tension between the
physical, spiritual and metaphysical claims of individuality and
the claims of nation and country, which strain away from self,
the embrace of society is offered as an essential form of whole-
ness—for those who can accept it. Ahmad seems at first to be
doomed to repeat the alienation of Kamal, fall into the pit
between body and spirit from which Kamal turns this way and
that to find The Concealed Side, encounter Zaabalawi. Ahmad
too, like Kamal, suffers a Proustian frustration of hopeless love;
but when, in his firm rejection of old privileges along with the
old chains of parental wishes, he refuses the chance to enter

government service and instead becomes a journalist on a pro-
gressive paper, he marries an emancipated girl and shares with
her the fulfilment of sexual love and idealistic commitment.

A prosaic solution?

A union Kamal is never to achieve.

While Kamal ends up, in his father's definition, 'as an unmarried teacher and an emotionally crippled recluse', life capri-
ciously, cruelly, offers him another chance. At extra-mural
classes in philosophy with which he is filling his empty leisure,
he sees a young student whose face surfaces from the painful,
treasured past. She is Budur, the baby sister of Aïda, grown up
and returned from abroad; he does not know that Aïda is dead,
yet it does seem that his dead love has arisen to offer itself.

He courts the girl within the old conventions as ardently as
his inhibitions will allow. '"See how she's brought you to life"
he reflected.' In the past, 'importance had been ascribed only
to sterile puzzles, like the will in Schopenhauer, the absolute
in Hegel, or the *élan vital* in Bergson. Life as a whole was
inanimate and unimportant. "See how a glance, a gesture, or a
smile can make the earth tremble today."'

When the girl responds by breaking convention and making
a move towards him—he turns away. He cannot tell her he
loves her, he cannot marry. (Shades of Kafka and Felice.) His
new friend Riyad chides him: 'How could breaking off with
her have seemed so trivial to you after you have been talking
of her as the girl of your dreams?'

'She was not the girl of his dreams, for that girl would never
have him.'

So Mahfouz stuns, as he can do so often, with what *is not
written,* what develops as if from invisible ink between the lines
of his text: she was not Aïda.

Kamal's failure to fulfil the girl's anticipation of his declaration of love was not missing his chance; it was unconscious revenge for her sister's spurning of him.

It would be fashionably easy to decide that Kamal is a repressed homosexual and his destructive despair comes from this. Certainly, his only ease and sense of belonging comes in friendships with male intellectuals, in ironic balance with his father's relationship with the libertine companions of brothel parties.

But Kamal's crucifying dichotomy between romantic idealism and sex would seem to be the more likely explanation for his sexual behaviour, just as the dichotomy between political action and the quest for Zaabalawi, The Concealed Side, would seem to be the best explanation for his inability to act upon or within society in a way meaningful to him. He has his regular nights: 'he and his favourite prostitute had reached the same point in life—that of a person whose life was not worth living.' And yet: 'Inside him there was also something that made him shy away from the notion of a passive escape from life . . . the fact that he clung to the agitated rope of life with both hands contravened his lethal skepticism.'

The agitated rope of life is suspended, in this epoch, over the outcome of the 1939–45 war. Human life going up in the smoke of incinerators, mushroom clouds—this war is of concern in the alternative world of Palace Walk, Palace of Desire and Sugar Street only when the German army is on the outskirts of Alexandria. The concentration camps and atom bombs have no place in the consciousness reflected here. However shocking this may be to Euro-Americans, the fact is that the meaning of victory on one side or the other, for a land weary of colonial occupation, is only bitter speculation of which master would be less intolerable, the unknown German or the familiar hated English.

Belonging to the generation which demonstrates the political polarisation inherent in differing opposition to whichever ideology represents the occupying colonial power and the monarchy it supports as a front, the brothers Ahmad and Abd al-Muni'm are arrested at the end of the war. Both, from opposing ideological positions, threaten the monarchy of King Faruk.

In a cell with common criminals, Abd al-Muni'm the Muslim extremist asks: 'Am I cast into this hole merely because I worship God?'

And Ahmad the Communist whispers mischievously: 'What could my offense be, then, since I don't.'

Ahmad, deserter of his past, of his class, of religious and secular submission, reflects nevertheless on how he had often written about 'the people' in his beautiful study on Sugar Street. Now

Here they were—cursing or snoring in their sleep . . . he had seen their wretched sullen faces, including that of the man who was scratching his head and armpits. At this very moment his lice might be advancing resolutely toward Ahmad and his brother. 'You are devoting your life to people like this' he told himself. 'Why should the thought of contact with them worry you? . . . our human condition has united us in this dark and humid place: the Muslim Brother, the Communist, the drunkard and the thief' . . . the heavy glowering prison gates would always hover at the horizons of his life . . . What distinguishes man from all other creatures if not his ability to condemn himself to death by his own free will?

At the point at which Naguib Mahfouz closes his work, Ahmad Abd al-Jawad, the sensual life-force of the patriarchal past, is spent, dead, and Amina the quietist, who at her daily coffee-hour held the conflicting currents of individual will within change, is dying; Abd al-Muni'm's baby is born while he and his brother Ahmad are in a prison camp, sentenced for subversion.

If the way to truth is to be able to risk one's life for it, 'to condemn oneself to death by one's own free will', Kamal will never reach The Concealed Side.

Is his salvation that he knows it? Is that enough? He doubts that, too. 'Mysticism is an evasion of responsibilities and so is a passive faith in science. There is no alternative to action, and that requires faith. The issue is how we are to mold for ourselves a belief system that is worthy of life . . . The choice of a faith has still not been resolved. The greatest consolation I have is the fact that the struggle is not over yet. It will be raging even when, like my mother's, my life has only three more days remaining.' He quotes to his friend Riyad what Ahmad said after he visited him in prison: 'I believe in life and in people . . . I also see myself compelled to revolt against ideals I believe to be false, since recoiling from this rebellion would be a form of treason. This is the meaning of perpetual revolution.'

In the last pages, Kamal, walking in the streets of Cairo with his brother Yasin, encounters a familiar figure from Palace Walk, an old blind shaykh, calling out to passersby, 'Which way to paradise?' Someone laughs: 'First turn to your right.'

Egypt at the period of these final pages has not yet overthrown the monarchy, the revolution is not yet accomplished. The African ethos is not yet recognized in Egypt, by Egypt. The day when Egypt will be part of the Organization of African Unity is distant, still to come. The day when Arab and Jew will have common borders is near, still to come. But 'Art is the interpreter of the human world,' claims one of Mahfouz's personages. There will be works of fiction where the search for Zaabalawi of Kamal and Ahmad will be carried on in existential situations akin to theirs, whether by apposition or opposition. Nearly half a century after the closing pages of Mahfouz's trilogy are dated, the quest in the alternative world by alternative writers goes on for the Home that is truth, undefined by walls, by borders, by regimes. It is pursued in, among others, the fiction of the Nigerian Chinua Achebe and the Israeli Amos Oz.

4

To Hold the Yam and the Knife
Anthills of the Savannah

CHINUA ACHEBE

Kamal's Egypt in *The Cairo Trilogy* of Naguib Mahfouz has emerged from generations of foreign occupations finally about to be overthrown in revolution.

Kangan, the West African country of three British-educated boyhood friends, Sam, Ikem and Chris, in Chinua Achebe's novel *Anthills of the Savannah,* has achieved independence through gentlemanly Lancaster House–type negotiations with the single foreign occupation it has known.

Power has dropped from the dying British imperial grasp. The yam and the knife are in the hands of the indigenous people themselves. And already the yam—sustenance and privilege—and the knife—authority imposed by army and police—have been snatched from the civilian government of independence by a military coup. If Kangan has been spared revolutionary struggle for its freedom from colonial rule, it has known the irony of a civil war as a consequence of freedom.

But if Chinua Achebe, writing his novel during the years his own country, Nigeria, has lived under military rule, has given his country a fictional name it cannot be as a precaution against personal arraignment for subversion, for he has risked and suffered this fearlessly before. It is because what he has seen and sees taking place in other African states, as well as what he knows in his own, demands that the responsibility of this knowledge be placed upon him to *go too far:* which is to confront himself and his people with what he has learnt of the truth about themselves.

The Concealed Side entered here is a terrain whose un-mapped natural features have a political rather than a metaphysi-cal formation, but cannot be therefore comfortably dismissed as native to Africa and exotic to any other country and society outside that continent.

The yam and the knife may be called by other names else-where—perhaps the stock exchange and the Mafia—but to hold yam and knife is the overwhelming motive of national and societal behaviour, East and West, North and South, First World and all other internationally designated worlds.

Achebe goes far and deep into the consequences.

Not only in the musical-chairs game of politics under differ-ent ideological pretexts, where the privileged change seats with one another, Presidents taking the Governors', coup colonels taking over the Presidents' seat of power, local racketeers taking over that of the foreign exploiters. Ikem the poet and newspa-per editor, Chris the Commissioner for Information under Sam become His Excellency the President, Beatrice, Chris's English-university-educated lover—all are set by Achebe to unravel, within themselves, the extent to which they are compromised by the new hierarchy of privilege, their very awareness of the pain and poverty of their people a kind of luxury in itself.

Self-questioning is the first signpost in the search for

Zaabalawi—The Concealed Side—encountered in Mahfouz's *Cairo Trilogy.*

Ikem interrogates himself about social attitudes in his post-colonial country: 'How does the poor man retain his calm . . . From what bottomless wells of patience does he draw? His great good humour must explain it. This sense of humour turned sometimes against himself must be what saves him from total dejection. He had learnt to squeeze every drop of enjoyment he can out of his stony luck. And the fool who oppresses him will make a particular point of that enjoyment: *You see, they are not in the least like ourselves. They don't need and can't use the luxuries that you and I must have. They have the animal capacity to endure the pain of, shall we say, domestication.*'

Ah yes, here is the prototype black-face of Western tradition whose features, there, changed first to the fear-inspiring mask of Black Power and now have become the icon of international salvation that is the face of Mandela.

But Achebe turns the demeaning shame of the tradition surviving in the new inheritors of the yam and the knife on the African middle class itself, concluding that these are 'The very words the white master had said in his time about the black race as a whole. Now we say them about the poor.'

And he takes the truth to be found in paradox still further—to the conditioned snobbery of the poor, their admiration for the

undeserved accoutrements of those who oppress them . . . how does one begin to explain the down-trodden drivers' wistful preference for a leader driving not like themselves in a battered and spluttering vehicle but differently, stylishly in a Mercedes and better still with another down-trodden person like them-

72

selves for a chauffeur? Perhaps a root-and-branch attack would cure that diseased tolerance too, a tolerance verging on admiration by the trudging jigger-toed oppressed for the Mercedes-Benz-driving, private-jet-flying, luxury-yacht-cruising oppressor. An insistence by the oppressed that his oppression be performed in style! What half-way measures could hope to cure that? No, it had to be full measure, pressed down and flowing over! Except that in dictatorships of the proletariat where roots have already been dug up and branches hacked away, an atavistic tolerance seems to linger . . . for the stylishness of dachas and special shops etc. for the revolutionary elite.

Even Ikem's lover, Elewa, daughter of a market woman, is 'sharply and decisively' on the side of her people in these distorted values. Of Ikem's old jalopy she says reproachfully: 'I no tell you that before, say this kind car wey you get de make person shame. Today he no get battery, tomorrow him tyre burst. I done talk say if you no want bring money for buy better car why you no take one good Peugeot from office as others de do and take one driver make he de drive am for you? . . . Me I no understand am-o.'

Islam is a way of life (as Abd al-Muni'm preaches) that cannot be followed by an unbeliever. Whereas Kamal's alienation from the Egyptian people—the rare moments of identification with whom bring him to life—comes from his rejection, in favour of materialist philosophy and Western humanism, of the traditional religion and its customs which, at least, the middle-class family of Mahfouz's *Cairo Trilogy* and the beggars and street venders of Cairo share, Ikem's, Chris's and Beatrice's variation of the state of alienation comes only from the difference made by Western education, mores, and economic status between them and the men and women of Gelegele market.

❦

They retain, ready to be tapped, access to the sturdy traditions of African life; the wry wisdom of its proverbs, the earthy philosophy of its legends, its myths of creation which survive as poetic secular guidance although the religious beliefs that created them have been abandoned or buried under Christianity. One way of reading Achebe's novel is to see this access to the past as worthy of consideration as the saving contradiction of the 'alienated history' of a colonized people. But Achebe will not have it relied upon or romanticized. Like other possibilities, it is there to be explored, hand over hand, on a precarious life-line.

Characterising himself and his two friends, Ikem and Sam, Chris recalls the song of a childhood game: The one in the front spots evil spirits, the one at the rear has twisted hands, the one in the middle is the child of luck.

Ikem, editor of the *National Gazette*, perilously exposing government corruption and the brutal self-corruption arisen in the people to complement it, is the one who spots evil spirits.

Sam, Sandhurst-trained, His Excellency the President, is the one with twisted hands, manoeuvring power.

Chris casts himself as the man in the middle, the child of luck, 'neither as bright as Ikem nor such a social success as Sam.'

But if he is the child of luck he is also his old boyhood friend's, the President's, appointee, his Commissioner for Information; he is there in the independence version of the colonial Old Boy network, a lackey expected to do the President's bidding without question, and in turn to pass on that bidding to the third member of the Old Boy triumvirate, Ikem, counted upon to see that the government gets a good press.

A delegation of elders from the northern province, Abazon, arrives in the capital and, swelled by its people who have been drawn to the city to find work, marches to the Presidential Palace with the intention of presenting a petition. Abazon is in the President's disfavour because in a referendum the province voted 'no' to making the presidency a life appointment. He has retaliated by halting a promised scheme to improve the water supply in their parched province. The delegation has come to request him to restore work on their wells. It is easy enough to get some functionary to fob off these simple people: a pressing engagement of state prevents the President from meeting the delegation. But although they are of no account, their fruitless pilgrimage must not be interpreted by the public as a protest demonstration turned away—all must be seen to be rosy in Kangan.

In the course of a bitingly comic cabinet meeting (one of Achebe's potent weapons against corruption in power is to make those who practise it reveal that evil is not only banal, it also may be ridiculous) Chris is summoned to instruct Ikem to send a photographer to a reception and report it as held in welcome for an Abazonian goodwill delegation, come to pay homage to the President.

The contradiction inherent in the role Chris and Ikem have intended to play in the triumvirate, letting Sam 'glimpse a little light now and again through chinks in his solid wall of court jesters', and the positions they hold in his grasp, swiftly takes control of the narrative when Ikem, himself by ancestry an Abazonian, 'for reasons of his own, in search of personal enlightenment' goes to meet the leaders of the Abazon delegation at a sleazy hotel in the city slums where they have gathered to drink and discuss their aborted visit to the Palace.

In a flash-back later in the novel Ikem reflects that he has thought of his tongue-in-cheek sycophancy before the President as 'a game that began innocently enough and then went suddenly strange and poisonous . . . If I am right . . . it should be possible to point to a specific event and say: it was at such and such a point that everything went wrong. But I have not found such a moment or such a cause although I have sought hard and long for it.'

Achebe has the great storyteller's gift of *letting the reader* discover the event and the moment. A full account of what takes place at the hotel is held back, in the narrative, to be revealed only half-way through the novel. But contexts, for the reader, grow, in a progression of interruptions and interludes more meaningfully cumulative than any chronology, towards discovery of the event that at once epitomises what has gone wrong and precipitates the extraordinary resorts of courage and cunning in thought and action that attempt to prevail against it.

An old man of Abazon makes a speech:

> . . . shifting-eyes people came and said: Because you said no to the Big Chief he is very angry and has ordered all the water bore-holes they are digging in your area closed so that you will know what it means to offend the sun . . . So we came to Bassa to say our own yes and perhaps the work on our bore-holes will start again and we will not all perish from the anger of the sun. We did not know before but we know now that *yes* does not cause trouble. We do not fully understand the ways of today yet but we are learning. A dancing masquerade in my town used to say: It is true I do not hear English but when they say Catch am nobody tells me to take myself off as fast as I can. So we are ready to learn new things . . . Sometime ago we were told that the Big Chief himself was planning to visit our villages and see our suffering. Then we were told again that he was not

coming because he had just remembered that we had said no to him two years ago. So we said, if he will not come, let us go and visit him instead in his house. It is proper that a beggar should visit a king. When a rich man is sick a beggar goes to visit him and says sorry. When the beggar is sick, he waits to recover and then goes to tell the rich man that he has been sick. It is the place of the poor man to make a visit to the rich man who holds the yam and the knife. Whether our coming to the Big Chief's compound will do any good or not we cannot say . . . But we can go back to our people and tell them that we have struggled for them with what remaining strength we have . . .

And the old man tells a story:

Once upon a time the leopard who had been trying for a long time to catch the tortoise finally chanced upon him on a solitary road.

Aha, he said, *at long last! Prepare to die.*

And the tortoise said: *Can I ask one favour before you kill me?*

The leopard saw no harm in that and agreed.

Give me a few moments to prepare my mind the tortoise said.

Again the leopard saw no harm in that and granted it.

But instead of standing still as the leopard expected the tortoise went into strange action on the road, scratching with hands and feet and throwing sand furiously in all directions.

Why are you doing that? asked the puzzled leopard.

The tortoise replied: *Because even after I am dead I would want anyone passing by this spot to say, yes, a fellow and his match struggled here.*

My people, that is all we are doing now. Struggling. Perhaps to no purpose except that those who come after us will be able to say: *True, our fathers were defeated but they tried.*

And the old man gives a vigorously lyrical disquisition on the place of Ikem, the poet and writer, in the struggle for justice; one that may be claimed for all three writers, Mahfouz, Achebe and Oz.

> The sounding of the battle-drum is important; the fierce waging of the war itself is important; and the telling of the story, afterwards—each is important in its own way. I tell you there is not one we could do without. But if you ask me which of them takes the eagle-feather I will say boldly: the story. Do you hear? Now when I was younger, if you had asked me the same question I would have replied without a pause: the battle . . . So why do I say that the story is chief among his fellows? The same reason I think that our people will give the name Nkolika to their daughters—Recalling-Is-Greatest. Why? Because only the story can continue beyond the war and warrior. It is the story that outlives the sound of war-drums and the exploits of brave fighters. It is the story that saves our progeny from blundering like blind beggars into the spokes of the cactus fence.

Ikem has told that story—the story of corruption—in many critical editorials. The welcome he receives from the Abazon delegation offers a trumped-up opportunity for the President's Security Police to accuse him of fomenting an Abazonian rebellion.

The first move against him is the President's instruction to the Commissioner for Information, Chris, to dismiss Ikem from his editorship. Chris refuses and at once declares his own resignation as Commissioner for Information.

'Resignation! Ha ha ha ha ha. Where do you think you are? Westminster or Washington D.C.?'

The President's laughter is a threat; levity is power's contempt.

Ikem's determination is not the fanaticism of the holy war of religious edicts against the infidel, it is fanatical horror at the brutalization of abuse of power and the cheapening of cruelty, the deadening response of mindless violence habituation to oppression creates.

Present at a public hanging, Ikem has witnessed a paradigm of this and of his country's degradation. The common-thief victim shouts before the moment of execution, 'I shall be born again.' The crowd reacts in

a new explosion of jeers and lewd jokes and laughter . . . I knew then that if its own mother was at that moment held up by her legs and torn down the middle like a piece of old rag that crowd would have yelled with eye-watering laughter. I still ask myself how anyone could laugh at such a terrible curse or fail to be menaced by the prospect of its fulfilment. For it was clear to me that the robber's words spoken with such power of calmness into the multitude's hysteria just minutes before his white lace reddened with blood and his hooded head withered instantly and drooped to his chest were greater than he, were indeed words of prophecy. If the vision vouchsafed to his last moments was to be faulted in any particular it would be this: that it placed his reincarnation in the future when it was already a clearly accomplished fact. Was he not standing right there, full grown, in other stolen lace and terylene, in every corner of that disoriented crowd? And he and all his innumerable doubles, were they not mere emulators of those who daily stole more from us than mere lace and terylene? Leaders who openly looted our treasury, whose effrontery soiled our national soul.

Calling on the President to abrogate the law that permits such a revolting performance, Ikem had ended a crusading editorial with a verse to be sung to the tune of the hymn 'Lord Thy Word Abideth':

> The worst threat from men of hell
> May not be their actions cruel
> Far worse that we learn their way
> And behave more fierce than they.

To behave worse than the foreign masters; this is the accepted legacy of colonialism that, admitted by a country's writer, goes too far for national pride and his safety, just as his exposé of official corruption does.

So far as the President is concerned, in his association with the Abazon delegation Ikem has finally betrayed the Old-Boy network knit expressly to keep His Excellency off the common ground of the people's grievances and social disintegration. Television announces Ikem's dismissal from editorship of the *National Gazette* and the arrest of the Abazon men, including the old orator, who led the march on the Palace.

Ikem ignores the advice of Chris and Beatrice to lie low, and gives a lecture at the university. This defiance takes as theme the old man of Abazon's parable, 'The Tortoise and the Leopard', transformed as 'a political meditation on the imperative of struggle.'

Again Achebe, relentlessly after The Concealed Side of his Africa, without whose revelation it will never be healed, is not satisfied with a scene of obvious daring, inspiring youth to a panacea of orthodox Leftist revolt.

The phrase 'the imperative of struggle' is greeted with tumultuous applause.

'No doubt it had the right revolutionary ring to it, and Ikem smiled inwardly at the impending coup d'état he would stage against this audience and its stereotype notions of struggle.' The creed he proposes is not what the students complacently anticipated: he tells them: 'whatever you are is not enough, you must find a way to accept something however small from the other to make you whole and save you from the mortal sin of righteousness and extremism.' There must be a new radicalism 'clear-eyed enough to see beyond the present claptrap that will heap all our problems on the doorstep of capitalism and imperialism.'

Ikem wins over the audience at question time when, asked what he thinks of the current idea of putting the President's head on the local currency, he delights them by replying, 'My view is that any serving President foolish enough to lay his head on a coin should know he is inviting people to take it off; the head, I mean.'

Next morning his old newspaper blazons the headline: 'Ex-editor advocates regicide.'

Now he is accused of plotting subversion with neo-imperialist agents—an English friend summarily deported. He is abducted from his flat by Security Police in the middle of the night and reported as having tried to seize a policeman's gun and been shot in the ensuing scuffle—security-speak for doing away with a political opponent that everyone in a police or military state translates.

With Ikem's death the pace and prose of the novel change. The search for the significance of the events that follow swiftly must leave behind the marvellous discourse and soliloquy which have opened such broad spaces of humour and amplitude of ideas in the narrative; Achebe knows the different timing of tragedy.

Chris, who had the temerity to think he could resign his

❧

post, is next on the list of elimination of the Old Boys who have let down the President.

Chris goes into hiding—on the face of it, out of danger to himself—but for him because the 'overwhelming issue' of 'how to counter the hideous lie' about Ikem's death has come out of moral confusion to a clear purpose of his life; the meaning of his existence within a particular time and place which, in his revulsion from what it has become, has been 'his place that did not know him.'

Like Ikem, he has long felt the 'necessity . . . to connect his essence with earth and earth's people', those 'one thousand live theatres' of the people of the Gelegele market. Achebe creates the realization that to counter the lie in one's society is the final test of connecting that essence, the final test of freedom: Mahfouz's definitive freedom: from colonization, from absolute rule of any kind, in commitment to and within the condition, the close company, of fellow citizens.

Chris calls foreign correspondents to a secret meeting-place and broadcasts on the BBC the truth: that Ikem was murdered.

A student uprising results from his parable of the tortoise and the leopard. A student leader is on the run from the Security Police; Chris sets off with him to escape to the North by bus, in the person of a motor spares salesman, an ironic circumstantial guise of entering his essence with that of the people. Having trouble at road-blocks with comporting himself in the appropriate manner of a man of the people, he remarks in pidgin with the self-mockery which exhilarates Achebe's characters no matter what befalls them: 'To succeed as small man no be small thing.'

As the bus grinds and lurches into the landscape of the North picked bare by heat and drought, it meets a crowd gathered in the road. 'A road accident? No! There was something discernible in the prancing about which did not suggest sorrow or anger but a strange kind of merry-making. And now there was no longer any doubt. Beer bottles could be seen in nearly all hands and the dancing—for no other name seemed better for this activity—was constantly accompanied by the throwing of the head backwards and the emptying of bottles direct into gullets without touching the lips.'

On the police post radio the news has come of a coup: the President is overthrown and assassinated. At the time the news was received, a truck transporting beer came by and was commandeered in celebration by the locals.

From this bizarre bacchanal Chris never reaches Abazon, whose plight has been the point of no return for Ikem and for him in their separate ways of search through the thoroughfares, alleys and haunts, the traffic of lies, sycophancy and social disorientation, for Zaabalawi, The Concealed Side of truth. And he dies not in political struggle but stepping between a young girl, fellow bus passenger, and a drunk policeman who is about to rape her.

Like the death of Mahfouz's Fahmy, his death might seem to belong to the Absurd, something that drains the meaning out of struggle for justice, out of life itself. This death, what for? Yet it emerges, rippling in widening circles the concept of justice, whose ultimate meaning can come only out of absolute respect for the dignity of the humblest individual human life.

Chris did not die for a girl whose name he did not even know; he died because he had found what is worth living for.

These novels of the Other World—Egypt, Africa and Israel— can accommodate rhetoric that would break the spell of the imagination in most fiction. This is because politics and its language, in imagery, in allusion, in interpretation of daily life, are so pressing a part of everyday speech in this Other World. Early on in Achebe's novel, Ikem, who has an affinity with Chris's lover, Beatrice, that might have become a love affair, visits her and reads to her what he calls a love-letter to his country:

> The women are, of course, the biggest single group of oppressed people in the world and, if we are to believe the Book of Genesis, the very oldest. But they are not the only ones. There are others—rural peasants in every land, the urban poor in industrialized countries, Black people everywhere including their own continent, ethnic and religious minorities and castes in all countries. The most obvious practical difficulty is the magnitude and heterogeneity of the problem. There is no universal conglomerate of the oppressed. Free people may be alike everywhere in their freedom but the oppressed inhabit each their own peculiar hell. The present orthodoxies of deliverance are futile to the extent that they fail to recognize this . . . The simplistic remedies touted by all manner of salesmen . . . will always fail because of man's stubborn antibody called surprise. Man will surprise by his capacity for nobility as well as for villainy. No system can change that. It is built into the core of man's free spirit.

The 'love-letter' is a testament of a political and ethical philosophy foreshadowing (the novel was published in 1987) the reaction against political ideologies that was to come with the collapse of the Soviet empire and the vacuum left by the evanescence of the Cold War. The reaction was and is a paroxysm of revulsion, one might say, against *all* political ideologies except that loosest concept, democracy, open to many interpretations, which allows doubts and contradictions while it does not always risk deciding how to deal with these.

Ikem is vehemently for reform as against revolution—but then he has come out of the colonial situation by negotiation alone. His was unlike situations such as that exemplified in South Africa, where revolutionary tactics, including eventual violence, had to be employed by the indigenous people in order to end a savage white minority regime.

Ikem's concern is an internal post-colonial one, where revolution implies civil war of a different nature. He tells his country:

> Experience and intelligence warn us that man's progress in freedom will be piecemeal, slow and undramatic . . . Reform may be a dirty word then but it begins to look more and more like the most promising route to success in the real world . . . Society is an extension of the individual. The most we can hope to do with a problematic individual psyche is to re-form it . . . We can only hope to rearrange some details in the periphery of the human personality. Any disturbance of its core is an irresponsible invitation to disaster. Even a one-day-old baby does not make itself available for your root-and-branch psychological engineering, for it comes trailing clouds of immortality. What immortality? Its baggage of irreducible inheritance of genes . . . It has to be the same with society. You reform it around what it is, its core of reality; not around an intellectual abstraction.

Then comes the reprimand, with—as is common when liberalism discards the ideology of the Left without distinction along with that of the Right—no new theory of political formation to suggest. Ikem continues: 'None of this is a valid excuse for political inactivity or apathy. Indeed to understand it is an absolute necessity for meaningful action, the knowledge of it being the only protective inoculation we can have against false hopes and virulent epidemics of gullibility. In the vocabulary of certain radical theorists contradictions are given the status of some deadly disease to which their opponents alone can succumb. But contradictions are the very stuff of life.'

All writers suffer that lack of understanding of the creative imagination by which the views of fictional characters are attributed to the author. I have no intention of identifying Chinua Achebe with Ikem, knowing as I do, as a writer (without citing Flaubert), that he is at once both every personage, male and female, and none of them, in every novel he has written, whether compatible with or totally antipathetic as these personages might be to his own personality and convictions. But I think he might be ready to accept the exception that this love-letter of Ikem's could be his own love-letter to his country. We sometimes disagree with, are far removed from, the ideas of our characters, expounding them because such ideas exist in others; but sometimes we agree with them.

If this love-letter is indeed also Achebe's to his country, it reflects a deep distrust of Right and Left. It posits and pits the power of sheer human intelligence as the only effective weapon against the ultimate Super Power of lies and gullibility. Intelligence in all its avatars and contexts: as truth-as-information, as comprehension, as tolerance, as love—love in the sense in which Simone Weil once defined prayer as a particular form of intelligent concentration.

But as a novelist does not give answers but asks questions, is there a question embedded here?

A question for us to ask ourselves in this time of the forced retirement of political gods? What structure for 'meaningful action' do we have to house personal conscience; according to what plan that will translate the general good into action shall we re-form?

Democracy, with a pretty poor record in the form in which Western capitalism practised it upon countries like Kangan— can it reform itself appropriately and adequately for the needs of such countries, respecting that contradictions are the very stuff of life?

As Mahfouz's Ahmad, imprisoned victim of one politico-religious regime and having sober thoughts on the opposing political orthodoxy he has passionately embraced, says of political ideology, 'The choice of a faith has not been resolved.'

That Ikem delivers his love-letter—in a way more intimate than an erotic declaration—to Chris's lover, Beatrice, seems inexplicable in its place early on in the novel. But later it is perceived as having been a signal of the place Beatrice will come to take, central to the work, creating in the subtle unfolding of her symbiotic, syncretic personality, *artistic* unity out of the novel's contradictions, reforming it 'around what it is, its core of reality.'

For this is not a novel about three men as the protagonists and guardians of life. Running neither counter to them—nor in the dark shadow of male will and sexuality, as the women are in Mahfouz's *Palace Walk*—but in orchestration, as the voices of different instruments without which the full composition of existence cannot be heard or understood, are two women, Beatrice and Elewa.

It is easy to write them off as muses, obviously symbols of the new and old Africa. While both are native to their country, Beatrice is the African woman formed within colonial ideas of what human emancipation is, someone educated in an English university to whom Achebe in his early books would have referred as a 'been-to', and Elewa, Ikem's lover, is the illiterate daughter of one of the Gelegele market women.

But Achebe knows too much, has gone too far, to use any closed system of typology. These women break out of expectations of what they may be, each containing elements of the personality that might be attributed to the other. And it is not a simple matter of being sisters in the skin. It has more to do with responses to the shifting confrontations arranged by history, and by the process of forgetting and recalling by which we keep our balance in existence.

Beatrice Nwanyibuife is the child of colonial culture, who does not know 'the traditions and legends of her people' because 'they played but little part in her upbringing. She was . . . baptized and sent to schools which made much about the English and the Jews and the Hindu and practically everybody else but hardly put a word in for her forebears and the divinities with whom they had evolved. So she came to barely knowing who she was. Barely, we say, because she did carry a vague sense more acute at certain moments than others of being two different people.'

Beatrice does not know her people's explanations for the fact Achebe pays homage to in acknowledgement throughout his work: 'that we are surrounded by deep mysteries.'

She does not know her people's ontological myth, the concept of 'the moral nature of authority' connected to the life-giving existence of the Niger River as originating from 'the Pillar of Water sent down from the Almighty to join earth to the firmament of heaven.' She is ignorant of 'the mystery of metaphor to hint at the most unattainable glory by its very opposite, the most mundane starkness' by which it has come about that 'the indescribable Pillar of Water fusing earth to heaven' also became 'in numberless shrine-houses across the country, a dry stick rising erect from the bare earth floor.'

'But knowing or not knowing does not save us from being known and even recruited and put to work. For, as a newly-minted proverb among her [Beatrice's] people has it, baptism . . . is no antidote against possession by Agwu the capricious god of diviners and artists.' Ikem sees something in Beatrice others—including Chris, her lover—do not, and that she does not know is in herself. Ikem—slowly and beautifully becomes evident to the reader—laid before Beatrice his love-letter to his country because 'perhaps Ikem alone came close to sensing the village priestess who will prophesy when her divinity rides her, abandoning if need be her soup-pot on the fire.'

Perhaps it is also this sense of Beatrice that has made impossible with her a relationship of sexual love that would seem much more compatible, not to say likely, than Ikem's relationship with the pert little Gelegele market peasant, Elewa. Or are these cross-matings a form of instinctive attempt to become 'known by one's place'?

Elewa, not incidentally, provides Achebe with the opportunity to create, out of his own connection of 'his essence with earth and earth's people'—intact, never lost in exile, protected by a writer's inescapable naked sensibility to his or her origins— a woman of the people, light-hearted in her stoicism, capable in her poverty, lovable in the innocent shrewdness of her techniques of survival. She speaks the pidgin that Achebe grants her with humour and respect: his inside knowledge sets it apart from condescension or quaintness.

Elewa, ignorant of all but her own world, is *perfectly known to it*. She alone, of all the personages in the fiction of the Other

World I have chosen to speak of, effortlessly occupies this position on The Concealed Side the rest yearn for.

Yet isn't there a price to be paid for this, too?

She is not *known* to the computerised world whose interventions and trade agreements, the new gods of war and peace, hunger and plenty, the NATOs, GATTs, OPECs and Groups of 7, who will take charge of her life because no country in the twentieth and twenty-first century can exist, or wishes to, without them. How will her Gelegele market techniques of survival continue to serve her?

Writers ask questions, they do not give answers; with the exception that the future is always some sort of answer.

Elewa the Gelegele market girl carries Ikem the rebel intellectual's baby inside her: a living response to the contradictions in their mating, the contradictions in their country.

The future as a solution. The only one we have to offer?

The unborn child is the summons that Beatrice's unrecognized divinity, state of grace, makes to her, the been-to sophisticate, riding her not so much to abandon the soup-pot of Westernism, some of whose ingredients she will never cease to regard as essential intellectual elements which it is her people's right to appropriate to their own use, but to restore to the mix the nourishment, the bread of the yam strongly flavoured with the strength of tradition. Beatrice, so removed from Elewa in the past, takes Elewa in and cares for her in the fatalistic despair which overtakes the girl with the death of Ikem. But with the death of Chris, an exchange of dependency takes place, with Elewa calling upon stoical resources of her background to support Beatrice in her questioning grief: and out of this comes the synthesis of their human oneness, shedding like irrelevancies the differences in education and way of life.

⟨⟩

Beatrice, ridden by her divinity, takes charge of the future, adapting the traditional naming of the newborn baby to the realities of the present, for a start. In the absence of the child's father, she decides—with a touch of Western-acquired feminist 'empowerment' perhaps!—to perform the ceremony herself. There is an assembly of close friends:

> She picked up the tiny bundle from its cot and, turning to Elewa said: 'You name this child.'
>
> 'Na you go name am.'
>
> 'OK . . . Thanks. I will start afresh . . . There was an Old Testament prophet who named his son *The-remnant-shall-return.* They must have lived in times like this. We have a different metaphor, though; we have our own version of the hope that springs eternal. We shall call this child AMAECHINA: May-the-path-never-close. Ama for short.'
>
> 'But that's a boy's name.'
>
> 'No matter.'
>
> 'Girl fit answer am also.'
>
> 'It's a beautiful name. The Path of Ikem.'
>
> 'That's right. May it never close, never overgrow.'
>
> 'Das right!'
>
> 'May it always shine! The Shining Path of Ikem.'
>
> 'Dat na wonderful name.'
>
> 'Na fine name so.'
>
> 'In our traditional society,' resumed Beatrice, 'the father named the child. But the man who should have done it today is absent . . . Stop that sniffling, Elewa! The man is not here although I know he is floating around us now . . . I am used to teasing him and I will tease him now. What does a man know about a child anyway that he should presume to give it a name . . .'
>
> 'Nothing except that his wife told him he is the father,' said

Abdul, causing much laughter.

'Na true my brother,' said Braimoh. 'Na woman de come tell man say him born the child. Then the man begin make *inyanga* and begin answer father. Na *yéyé* father we be.'

'Exactly. So I think our tradition is faulty there. It is really safest to ask the mother what her child is or means or should be called. So Elewa should really be holding Ama and telling us what she is. What it was like to be loved by that beautiful man Ikem. But Elewa is too shy. Look at her!'

'I no shy at all,' she replied . . . 'I no shy but I no sabi book.'

'Dis no be book matter, my sister.'

'You no sabi book but you sabi plenty thing wey pass book, my dear girl' . . .

'All of we,' continued Beatrice, 'done see *baad* time; but na you one, Elewa, come produce something wonderful like this to show your sufferhead. Something alive and kicking.'

'But living ideas . . .' Emmanuel began haltingly.

'Ideas cannot live outside people,' said Beatrice . . .

'I don't accept that. The ideas in one lecture by Ikem changed my entire life from a parrot to a man . . . And the lives of some of my friends. It wasn't Ikem the man who changed me. I hardly knew him. It was his ideas set down on paper. One idea in particular: that we may accept a limitation on our actions but never, under no circumstances, must we accept restriction on our thinking.'

That is The Path of Ikem, with which the future has been endowed, something alive and kicking, coming out of the many paths that have been followed in the pursuit of Zaabalawi, The Concealed Side, in this novel.

As the 'anthills of the savannah survive to tell the new grass of last year's bush fires', the novel tells the story, the story of the land, whose story is its people. The old man of Abazon said: 'we all imagine that the story of the land is easy, that every one of us can get up and tell it. But that is not so.' It is Agwu who chooses his seers and diviners, and marks with the ring of white chalk the eye that makes the writer. 'In his [the writer's] newfound utterance', the old man says, 'our struggle will stand reincarnated before us. He is the liar who can sit under his thatch and see the moon hanging in the sky outside. Without stirring from his stool he can tell you how many commodities are selling in a distant marketplace. His chalked eye will see every blow in a battle he never fought.'

With his chalk-ringed eye Achebe grants Beatrice the possibility of having found The Concealed Side through becoming *known to her place*.

But from there he has opened up in her vision another savannah, forbidding, heat-haze- and mist-extended across her country, her continent, through which the Path of Ikem must search: 'The explanation of the tragedy of Chris and Ikem in terms of petty human calculation or personal accident had begun to give way in her throbbing mind to an altogether more terrifying but more plausible theory of premeditation. The image of Chris as just another stranger who chanced upon death on the Great North Road or Ikem as an early victim of a waxing police state was no longer satisfactory. Were they not in fact trailed travellers whose journeys from start to finish had been carefully programmed in advance by an alienated history? If so, how many more doomed voyagers were already in transit or just setting out, faces fresh with illusions of duty-free travel and happy landings ahead of them? . . . What must a people do to appease an embittered history?'

5

FORGOTTEN PROMISED LAND
Fima

AMOS OZ

> There is a forgotten promised
> land somewhere here—no, not a
> land, not promised, not even
> really forgotten, but something
> calling to you.

'What must a people do to appease an embittered history?'

Beatrice Nwanyibuife's cry in Achebe's *Anthills of the Savannah* winds through the streets of Jerusalem in Amos Oz's novel *Fima*. The Israeli Efraim Nisan—Fima—carries in the torn lining of his coat as he goes through his disorderly days in search of Zaabalawi—The Concealed Side of truth—both the embittered history, millennia of persecution, of the Jewish people, and the embittered history of their Occupation by conquest of land belonging to another people, the Palestinian Arabs.

It is surely one of the most ironic turns of history that a people cast out around the world for generations, without a homeland, should find themselves eventually in the position of a mini colonial power, determining the lives of others: where they have the right to live, what work they may do, what civil rights they shall have.

The moral conflict within his country's ethos has invaded

Fima's personality destructively, setting up an unceasing debate within him that extends obsessively to a kind of paralysis of the will to complete any task, whether this be changing his bed-sheets or writing an article on the very subject—his country's condition—that is burning him: an existential heartburn the antacid tablets he's always munching after indigestible snacks are powerless to appease.

Holding off what the day will bring, Fima lies in bed and records his dreams because he finds 'less falsehood in sleeping than in waking . . . he wanted to distance himself as much as possible from the petty lies that filled his everyday life like a fine dust that penetrated even to the most intimate crannies.' His is a contemporary Oblomovism, a kind of catatonic sense of powerlessness to do what you feel *you know must be done.*

In terms of national historical determinism, Fima's situation is the reverse of that of Ikem, in Achebe's *Anthills of the Savannah.* Ikem has been the product of colonization, not cast by his country in the role of colonizer; but they are brothers in their passion to shock their societies into self-realization of those societies' respective moral conditions.

Reading newspapers as he finally gets out of bed, Fima concludes of his Israel in 1989 'that the country has fallen into the hands of a bunch of lunatics, who went on and on about Hitler and the Holocaust and always rushed to stamp out any glimmer of peace, seeing it as a Nazi ploy aimed at their destruction.'

Ikem is prepared to go too far, in pursuit of truth against corruption in government and abuse of power; but corruption and abuse of power domestically, of his own government against its own people, are not the problem for Fima; it is his government's blind self-righteousness—the 'mortal sin of self-

95

righteousness' Ikem speaks of—against which Fima is impelled to go too far. Yet both are at one in revulsion from the tacit acceptance of violence in their societies, an acceptance of gross lies to which the sickening 'petty lies' of everyday life insidiously accustom society, those petty lies that bring bile also to the spirit of Naguib Mahfouz's Kamal, in *The Cairo Trilogy*.

Ikem is appalled by the spectacle of a public hanging in his country coming to be received by his people as entertainment. Fima is appalled by a different example of a society become unfeeling, persuaded into deadened consciousness of reality, this time by a kind of semantic cleansing.

On the midday news he heard that an Arab youth had been . . . killed that morning by a plastic bullet fired presumably from a soldier's rifle in the Jebeliyeh refugee camp in the course of a stone-throwing incident . . . He particularly disliked the expression 'killed by a plastic bullet'. And the word 'presumably' made him seethe . . . As if it's the plastic bullets that do the killing . . . He was angry, too, in a more general way, about the passive verbs that were beginning to take over official statements and seemed to be infecting the language as a whole.

But Fima's very state of being is a dialectic; maybe originating genetically in talmudic wandering for two thousand years in pursuit of Zaabalawi, The Concealed Side, yet certainly in his own time and circumstance the only possible response to the state of moral reversals, the trading of places between victim and perpetrator he sees in his contemporary society. He continues: 'Although, in fact, it might be a healthy and wholly laudable sense of shame that prevented us from announcing simply: a Jewish soldier has shot and killed an Arab teenager. On the other hand, this polluted language was constantly teaching us that the fault lay with the rifle, with the circumstances that were being investigated, with the plastic bullet.'

To rouse himself from any such soothing lie he resorts to what appears to be clowning; a desperate response. Aiming a fork at his own forehead he tries to guess what it feels like 'the instant the bullet pierces the skull and explodes . . . Is there a fraction, an atom of time in which, who knows, illumination arrives? The light of the seven heavens? When what has been dim and vague all your life is momentarily opened up before darkness falls? As though all those years you have been looking for a complicated solution to a complicated problem, and in the final moment a simple solution flashes out?'

But at this point Fima turns angrily on himself: 'Just stop fucking up your mind. The words "dim and vague" filled him with disgust.' Fima is searching for certainties while aware, as Ikem was, that contradictions are the very stuff of life and all certitude must be suspect.

Striking oneself on the forehead with a table fork in simulation of the bullet entering there is an example of the Chaplinesque means of coming to grips with reality to which Fima often resorts. Who knows if there may be nourishment in the metaphor of devouring an old shoe? Where society is perceived as devious, all angles of approach to possible truth may have to be tried. Fima is often a shambling ridiculous figure, makes of himself such in opposition to the senselessness and sophistry of much so-called rational behaviour. He is grubby and neglectful of his person. Is this self-abasement a form of castigation? Is it degeneracy, or some sign of the saint and prophet, removed from the conventions of self?

Fima has gone through the apprenticeship of vagrancy and profligacy that popularly is supposed to purge the soul in preparation for these higher states of grace and knowledge. He has had, in his youth, what his friends call his 'billy-goat year' with a series of peripatetic sexual adventures in different countries. To this Dionysiac period belongs his single collection of poetry, *The Death of Augustine and His Resurrection in the Arms of Dulcinea*—a title somehow combining spiritual and sexual preoccupations with the Absurd, like a clue to the esoteric crossword puzzle of his personality.

Now—it is Amos Oz's achievement that one believes in this work's existence and in Fima's friends' conviction that he is wasting extraordinary gifts as a poet because Oz, like Achebe, has his own rare and great gifts enabling him to create a character whose ideas, discourse, and use of language—in this instance a poet's original imagery, supra-normal powers of observation, lyricism and passion in playfulness with words—are those of a creatively gifted intellectual. Only a writer who is himself a poet and polymath intellectual can produce evidence that his fictional character is one. Lesser writers expect us to take their word for this—which is the measure of what they themselves lack . . . Here, there is evidence on every page that Fima, indeed, has the chalk ring of Agwu, Achebe's god of diviners and artists, round his eye.

After the billy-goat year, Fima has had an unsuccessful marriage to Yael, an aeronautical engineer who then married in America an academic in the same field and now lives with her new husband back in Israel.

Fima is not only a poet manqué, he is also a husband and father manqué: he yearns lustfully after his ex-wife, he is possessively attached to the small son of his ex-wife and her new husband. He lives on the perimeter of these and other married friends' lives. He dotes on them: which means that he takes the right to exploit them with the burden of his loneliness and inept helplessness in the routine demands of daily life, the right to keep them up half the night arguing over anything under the sun. He is taken care of by them in their fond exasperation—contradicted by belief in him—as best they can, even to the extent of allowing one of the wives to take charge of his sexual needs by, as he himself soberly muses, 'servicing him' every couple of weeks. And when she rises from his bed she tackles his filthy kitchen with zeal that, he grants, could 'transform Calcutta into Zurich.'

The early promise of his poetry has never been achieved; the power of his intellect has never been put to use in public activity, or in any company outside his small circle of faithful friends. He is a menial in his society, as a pacifist conscript in an army may refuse to rise above the lowest rank if he has to serve at all.

He has *chosen to fail* in the terms of success his society recognizes because he believes it has lost its way, turned from the search for Zaabalawi, The Path of Ikem, and taken one he will not follow. He works as a receptionist in a private abortion outfit disguised as a gynaecological clinic—itself an example of the lying euphemisms that fill his life with dust.

Fima is always compelled to go too far—to go in reference beyond the particularity with which any concern is being addressed, whether with others or in his dialectical dialogue with himself. He is a womanizer—when he gets the chance—but with an attitude towards women totally different from that of a Jawad or Yasin in *The Cairo Trilogy* of Mahfouz; his desire is to pleasure and console the woman rather than use her.

For him, what goes on at the abortion clinic opens exploration of the mystery one sex has for the other, their difference as the fundament of the divided self. 'What was the story that ended in this clinic? . . . What was the male shadow behind this or that woman? And the child that would not be born, what was it? What would it turn out to be?'

For Fima, to understand the truth of existence is to attempt to understand all forms of suffering, whether through military occupation, war, racial prejudice, lies, individual cruelties, and no matter how diverse these may be, to find where all wrongs are inextricably linked. Fima struggles

> between revulsion and the feeling that he ought to participate, at least in his imagination, in every form of suffering. Sometimes womanhood itself struck him as being a crying injustice, almost a cruel illness that afflicted half the human race and exposed it to degradations and humiliations that the other half was spared. But sometimes a vague jealousy stirred inside him . . . As though he had been cheated of some secret gift that enabled *them* to relate to the world in a way that was barred to him forever. The more he thought about it, the less he was able to distinguish between his pity and his envy . . . Then he was swept by a profound wave of pity for all men and women, as though the separation of the sexes was nothing but a cruel prank. He felt that the time had come to rise up and with sympathy and reason to do something to put an end to it.

But as with his other urges to take on cosmic tasks, the only means he can put his hand to are the humblest, even fatuous ones: all he can think of to do is fetch a glass of cold water for one of the women in the doctor's waiting-room.

The shoulder-shrugging or bitter humour with which Oz punctures Fima's fantasies, whether he's solving the universal problems of being or the problems of his own society and country, never trivializes their validity and the courage of Fima's anguish, but measures the magnitude of what he takes upon himself, dancing on the hot coals of his challenges for truth. How absurd, this shabby middle-aged David; but where are the others in his circle who will face Goliath with a catapult?

Fima's political mission is conveyed with a brilliant evasion of didacticism by having him summon sessions of an imaginary cabinet which, of course, he, out of his warring mixture of scepticism and idealism, heads.

> He visualized himself convening his cabinet for a midnight sitting. An old revolutionary sentiment from his days in the youth movement made him hold this meeting in a classroom in a run-down school . . . He himself, wearing a workman's jacket and threadbare trousers, would sit not at the teacher's desk but on the window-sill. He would paint a pitiless picture of the realities, startling the ministers with his portrayal of the impending disaster. Towards dawn he would secure a majority for a decision to withdraw all our armed forces, as a first step, from the Gaza Strip, even without an agreement. 'If they fire on our settlements, I'll bomb them from the air. But if they keep quiet, if they demonstrate that they are serious about peace, then we'll wait a year or two and open negotiations with them about the future of the West Bank.'

Let us remember that the period is 1989; much of what Fima fantasized, an apostasy then, is now a reality. Fima calls his cabinet together again in the same classroom:

> At the door he posted a burly sentry in khaki shorts, Arab headdress, and knitted cap. (A crazy, wistful mixture of what a combined personage, Arab-Israeli, would wear.) Some of his ministers sat on the bare floor at his feet, others leaned against the wall, which was covered with educational diagrams. In a

few well-chosen words Fima presented them with the need to choose between the territories conquered in '67 and our very identity . . . Before we won the Six Days War, he mused, the state of the nation was less dangerous and destructive than it is now. Or perhaps it wasn't really less dangerous, just less demoralising and less depressing. Was it really easier for us to face up to the danger of annihilation than to sit in the dock facing the accusation of international public opinion? The danger of annihilation gave us pride and a sense of unity, whereas sitting in the dock now is gradually breaking our spirit.

Next time he convenes his cabinet 'he stunned them all by announcing that he intended to fly to Tunis at dawn to address the Palestine National Council . . . The only condition for starting to negotiate would be the total cessation of violence on both sides.'

He proceeds to dole out cabinet posts to his friends. 'And from now on the cabinet would be renamed the Revolutionary Council. The revolutionary process would be completed within six months. By then peace would be established. And immediately thereafter we can all return to our occupations and no longer interfere in the work of the elected government. I myself shall withdraw into total anonymity. I shall change my name and disappear. Now let us disperse separately by side entrances.'

I shall change my name and disappear.

A piece of impatient, apocalyptic dreaming, crazy wishful-thinking, suddenly moves into another sphere. The words could be those of the saviour, the prophet, who has found and speaks the truth and at once withdraws into its mystery. For Zaabalawi is never *available,* some cabinet minister sitting in his office; he must be continually sought. These possibilities are always there in Amos Oz's vision, which is at once of human frailty and absurdity, and of human promise. If this novel is *his* love-letter to his country, it is the castigation born of passionate concern.

The dialectic does not take place solely within Fima's mind, his self-questioning and his fantasies. A number of other voices join in. One is that of his father, Baruch Nomberg, a beguiling, endearing character, worthy of Isaac Bashevis Singer, flamboyant as Mahfouz's Jawad, in his way.

At eighty-two Baruch spends his time sitting in cafés sipping sweet liqueurs in the company of attractive widows. His indiscriminate bountifulness takes the form of the contradictions which, Achebe's Ikem has said, are the very stuff of life. In the old man these suggest an obstinate belief in the existence of good underlying all human error. 'He saw no contradiction in backing traditional values in education while also funding a campaign for the prevention of religious coercion. He dispensed grants . . . to victims of violent crime and also for the rehabilitation of violent criminals.'

When he comes on one of his meddling, uninvited visits to his son, Fima

> could almost hear him humming a Hasidic folk tune to himself as he climbed the stairs . . . even sometimes when he was being spoken to, the old man would be constantly intoning the characteristic ya-ba-bam . . . Fima could also almost sniff his father's special smell wafting up the stairs, that smell he remembered from his infancy . . . the scent of airless rooms, old furniture, steaming fish stew and boiled carrots, feather beds and sticky liqueur. Father and son exchanged a perfunctory em-

brace, this Eastern European aroma aroused in Fima a revulsion mixed with shame at the revulsion, together with the long-standing urge to pick a quarrel with his father, to trample on some sacrosanct principle of his.

Like Jawad—the two traditionalists, Arab and Jew—Baruch is a great talker, worried, as Jawad was about Kamal, that his son Fima is not leading a conventional life with marriage, children and a career. 'I asked that you should put a little order in your life. That you should be a *mensch*. That you should worry about the future for a change instead of worrying night and day about your beloved Arabs.'

'Only connect,' Forster said long ago, of human relations; and this holds good for levels of human preoccupation, as well. Here, as always in this immensely skilled work, the connection between the personal and the societal, the continuity and unity, the interdependence of these concepts comes swiftly.

> 'I'm not,' Fima corrected him, 'worried about the Arabs. I've explained to you a thousand times. I'm worried about us.'
>
> 'Of course Efraim, of course. Nobody can impugn the integrity of your motives. The sad thing is, the only people you manage to take in are yourselves. As though your Arabs are just asking nicely and politely if they can have Nablus and Hebron back, and then they'll go home happily ever after, peace be upon Israel and upon Ishmael. But that's not what they want from us . . . To slit our throats a little bit, that's all they want. To wipe us out.'

Fima explodes in a 'wounded roar': 'Baruch, you are blind and deaf. Open your eyes. We're the Cossacks now, and the Arabs are the victims of the pogroms, yes, every day, every hour.'

And his father comes back with: '. . . So what's wrong with us being the Cossacks for a change? Where does it say in Holy Scripture that Jew and Gentile are forbidden to swap jobs for a little while? Just once in a millennium or so?'

Waiting in a café for a rendezvous with a woman, Fima is approached by a young bearded activist from the Jewish settlements in the Territories, who mistakes him for someone else.

'We've arranged to meet someone we've never seen. I thought perhaps it was you. I'm sorry.'

'I'm not,' Fima declared forcefully, as though firing the first shot in a civil war, 'one of you. I think you're all a plague.'

The young man, with an innocent, sweet smile and a look suggesting Jewish solidarity, said:

'Why not save expressions like that for the enemy?'

Unable to concentrate on the woman, Fima broods on the incident. 'In the middle of the day, in broad daylight, in the middle of Jerusalem, they're already walking around with guns in their belts. Was the sickness implicit in the Zionist idea from the outset? Is there no way for the Jews to get back onto the stage of history except by becoming scum?'

Like Kamal, Fima spares no one. Walking through Jerusalem alone at night, he looks up at the lit staircases of the bourgeoisie. 'Automatic living, he thought, a life of comfort and achievement, accumulating possessions, honours, and the routine of eating, mating, and financial habits of prosperous people, the soul sinking under folds of flesh, the rituals of social position . . . This was the contented mind that had no dealing with death and whose sole concern was to remain contented.'

As for the government, 'If he were Prime Minister, he would make each member of the Cabinet stay for a week with a reserve unit in Gaza or Hebron, spend some time inside the perimeter of one of the detention camps in the Negev, live a couple of days in a run-down psycho-geriatric ward, lie in the mud and rain for a whole winter's night from sundown to dawn by the electronic fence on the Lebanese border . . .'

Fima spares no one; least of all himself.

And how about you, my dear Prime Minister? What have you ever done? What did you do today? Or yesterday? . . . And how you hated that young settler, who, after all, even when you make allowances for the stupidity of the government and the blindness of the masses, has no choice but to carry a gun, because he really does risk his life driving at night between Hebron and Bethlehem. What do you want him to do—stick his neck out to be slaughtered? . . . Everywhere we go, we leave behind us a trail of lifeless words, from which it is only a short way to the corpses of Arab children killed daily in the Territories. A short way too, to the unpalatable fact that a man like me simply erases from the register of the dead, without thinking, the children of the family of settlers burned alive the day before yesterday by a Molotov cocktail on the road to Alfei Menashe. Why did I erase them? Was their death insufficiently innocent? Unworthy to enter the shrine of suffering of which we have, as it were, made ourselves the guardians? Is it just that the settlers frighten and infuriate me, whereas the Arab children weigh on my conscience? Can a worthless man like me have sunk so low as to make a distinction between the intolerable killing of children and the not-so-intolerable killing of children?

Beneath his offensive and defensive struggles in the agonizing address of himself to his people, there is a level of understanding too deep for prolixity, unspeakable—even for the garrulous man of the word, Fima. It can find expression only through the compression of metaphor and parable, as with the meeting of the Tortoise and the Leopard, in Achebe's novel, where creatures humankind considers itself superior to stand for and are at one with the 'superior' in a continuum of the definitive experience—the curse?—of suffering and causing suffering. As always with Fima, what occurs sends the balance of human feeling swinging up and down between a weight of bedevilling aggressive instincts and the capacity for awe at the miracles of existence itself that persists inside him despite his disillusion and scepticism. And the awe is emphasized rather than defused by laughter; humour becomes a grace.

In his kitchen Fima happens upon a lodger.

Suddenly a cockroach came strolling towards him, looking weary and indifferent. It did not try to escape. At once Fima was fired with the thrill of the chase . . . he slipped off a shoe and brandished it, then repented as he recalled that it was just like this, with a hammer blow to the head, that Stalin's agents murdered the exiled Trotsky. And he was startled to discover the resemblance between Trotsky in his last pictures and his father, who had been here a moment before, begging him to marry. The shoe froze in his hand. He observed with astonishment the creature's feelers, which were describing slow circles. He saw masses of tiny stiff bristles, like a moustache. He studied the spindly legs seemingly full of joints. The delicate formation of the elongated wings. He was filled with awe at the precise, minute artistry of this creature, which no longer seemed abhorrent but wonderfully perfect; a representative of a hated race, persecuted and confined to the drains, excelling in the art of stubborn survival, agile and cunning in the dark; a race that had fallen victim to primeval loathing born of fear, of simple cruelty, of inherited prejudices. Could it be that it was precisely the evasiveness of this race, its humility and plainness, its powerful vitality, that aroused horror in us? Horror at the murderous instinct that its very presence excited in us? Horror because of the mysterious longevity of a creature that could neither sting nor bite and always kept its distance? He replaced the shoe on his foot, ignoring the rank smell of his sock. And he closed the door of the cupboard under the sink gently, so as not to alarm the creature.

The hated race, persecuted and confined, is Fima's own. He is himself the cockroach; and so are the blacks, and at his moment in history, in the Occupied Territories, the Palestinians. And he himself, in all the inescapable connections, the synapses to the neurons of existence, is the hater, the persecutor, the one with the hammer, the raised shoe.

A blind beggar in the streets of Mahfouz's Cairo calls out: 'Which way to paradise?'

Wandering in the streets of Jerusalem, Fima attracts the attention of a suspicious policeman who asks, 'Hey are you looking for something?' Fima replies, 'Yes. I'm looking for tomorrow.' The policeman politely suggests: 'Well, go along and look for it somewhere else, sir. Move along please. You can't wait here.'

For the present, Fima is in a city where

> Once upon a time kings and prophets, saviours, world reform-ers, madmen who heard voices, zealots, ascetics and dreamers walked . . . And one day in the future, in a hundred years or more, new men, totally different from us would be living here. Earnest, self-contained people. No doubt they would find all our troubles weird, unintelligible, perplexing. Meanwhile, and

for the time being, between the past and the future, we have been sent to inhabit Jerusalem. The city has been entrusted to our stewardship. And we fill it with oppression, foolishness and injustice. We inflict humiliation, frustration, torture on each other, not out of arrogance but merely from laziness and fear. We pursue good and cause evil. We seek to comfort and instead we wound. We aim to increase knowledge, and instead we increase pain . . . The crime *is* the punishment.

Where is the way to tomorrow, The Path of Ikem that will lead to The Concealed Side? The Path, The Concealed Side beckon in different guises to different individuals. Fima has sometimes found that sleep seemed less tainted with falsehood than waking, and at other times that 'ultimate wakefulness' was what he was after. He reaches the thought 'that it might be a matter of three states, not two . . . There is no more tragic loss, he thought, in the whole world than missing the Third State. It happens because of business, because of hollow desires and the pursuit of vanities and trivia. All suffering, Fima said to himself, everything that is ridiculous or obscene, is purely the consequence of missing the Third State, or of that vague nagging feeling that reminds us from time to time that there is, outside and inside, almost within reach, something fundamental that you always seem on the way to yet you always lose your way. You are called, and you forget to go. You are spoken to, and you don't hear.'

Once, in the sleeping state, Fima had a dream in which he was called and led by an unknown individual through a labyrinth of streets, alleys and courtyards in what was both Valladolid in Spain and the Bukharian Quarter of Jerusalem. This incarnation of Zaabalawi is in the personage of a woman. The woman says Fima is the father of her daughter. The woman is

109

cold; when he hugs her to warm her, her body shakes with despair, and she whispers "'Don't be afraid, Efraim, I know a way and I'll get you across to the Aryan side." In the dream this whispered phrase was full of promise and grace, and I continued to trust her and follow her ecstatically, and was not at all surprised when in the dream she turned into my mother, nor did I ask where the Aryan side was. Until we reached the water. At the water's edge, with a blond military moustache and legs spread wide, stood a man in a dark uniform who said: Have to separate.'

This is the old nightmare that attends the nights of Jews, a collective haunting by the cattle transports, the orderly camp reception: Have to separate. In the context of the Holocaust there is the obvious: the Aryan Side is the side of safety to which, by race, you cannot belong.

Have to separate. The decree also stands eternally in the air above the dark hole giving onto the sea through which at Gorée, an island off the coast of Senegal, Africans—wives taken from husbands, children from parents—took their last step from their land to the slave ships. But in its dream transformation the Aryan Side becomes a destination beyond evil discriminations by race, its meaning is vast, cast at large from the racist moorings of what it once was; the Aryan Side is a *destination,* it is *the place that knows you,* the Third State, The Concealed Side, that is reconciled with you, and can be so only in truth.

One of Fima's fantasies brings to life a student who would live in Fima's shabby apartment a century from his own day.

'He could see him in his mind's eye standing at this same window and staring out at those same hills. And he said to him: Don't you mock. It's thanks to us that you're here.' And he tells the student about a tree-planting ceremony when the mayor

❧

told assembled schoolchildren: you are the trees, and we are the manure. He visualizes the student living a universal life where there will be 'No more filthy kitchens, no more . . . cockroaches . . . The winter rain will have been swept away from Jerusalem forever. It will be diverted to the agricultural regions. Everyone will be taken across safely to the Aryan side, as it were.'

It takes the Jew, Fima, to transform the Aryan Side thus; one of Amos Oz's sleight-of-hand ironies, his own magic realism: of a kind that founds no school, being more difficult to imitate than the recognized one.

❧

If Fima were the author of Amos Oz's novel, that would be his form of action-in-being. But as he is not, he is one 'written about', we must look at his life in different terms. He thinks therefore he is. That is all. It is his sole accounting for his being. He is unlike Ikem, Chris and Beatrice of *Anthills of the Savannah,* unlike Abd al-Muni'm and Ahmad of *The Cairo Trilogy,* all of whom act as well as meditate upon their kind of convictions in their pursuit of Zaabalawi; he is brother to Kamal of the trilogy, consumed inwardly by fire as Kamal is consumed by melancholy.

In conflict with the way their respective countries, societies, peoples deal with the inherited mis-shapings of history, the tangle of good and evil in beliefs and traditions that have survived history and either stifle or succour, and the conduct of the present in which the future is predicated—all these personages, each attached to nowhere else in the world, are yet each living in the state that first came into Fima's head as 'his place does not know him.'

111

❧

It is a place that will not face the truth about itself, will not recognize its sons and daughters who are in search of Zaabalawi, The Concealed Side, to know and heal; 'To grasp' (as Fima puts it) 'as much as we can, or at least to grasp our inability to grasp.'

Fima sometimes pictures 'the creator of the universe, in whom he did not entirely believe, in the form of a Jerusalem tradesman of Middle Eastern origin', and he might as easily be pictured, with a change of a few appurtenances, as a Cairo tradesman in the Khan al-Khalili bazaar, a vender in the Gelegele Market, a stall-holder in a London flea market or an American fairground. Or could he be Zaabalawi himself?

Fima sees this man

aged about sixty, lean and tan and wrinkled, eaten away by cigarettes and arak, in threadbare brown trousers and a not very clean white shirt buttoned right up to his skinny neck but without a tie, and with worn-out brown shoes and a shabby old-fashioned jacket a little too small for him. This creator sat drowsily on a wicker stool, facing the sun, his eyes half-closed, his head sunk on his chest, in the doorway of his haberdashery shop . . . A dead cigarette-end hung from his lower lip and a string of amber beads was frozen between his fingers, where a broad ring flashed from time to time. Fima stopped and dared to address him, with exaggerated politeness, in the third person, hesitantly: Might I be permitted to disturb Your Worship with just one question? A twitch of irony flitted across the wrinkled, leathery face. Perhaps just a fly buzzing? Would Your Worship deign to consider the Brothers Karamazov? The argument be-tween Ivan and the Devil? Mitya's dream? Or the episode of the Grand Inquisitor? No? And what would Your Worship deign to reply to that question, *Vanity of Vanities*? Would Your Worship resort again to the old arguments: *Where wast thou when*

❧

I laid the foundation of the world? I am that I am. The old man released a kind of belch reeking of tobacco and arak, turned up his two palms, which were pitted as a plasterer's, and spread them empty on his knees. Only the ring on his finger glimmered for a moment and then faded. Was he chewing something? Smiling? Dozing? Fima abandoned his quest. Apologising, he went on his way. Not running, not hurrying, yet nevertheless like one who is running away and knows he is, and also knows that running away is useless.

Old *bon viveur* Baruch, Fima's father, dies, and Fima, the man who distrusts possessions as obstructions in the way to The Concealed Side, finds he has inherited a thriving cosmetics factory. Vague stirrings that he ought to do some good with it in the way society tolerates philanthropy that does not disturb the ethos of power—look into the welfare of the workers, etcetera—give way as he goes through Baruch's luxurious apartment, with its bathtub on brass lion's paws and its collection of silver snuff boxes decorated with pearls. This too, his father has laid upon him. Could he accept this life, move in? '. . . all those exciting objects . . . insisted on concealing from him the thing that really mattered . . . and he said to himself: "Right. Exile."'

He cannot reconcile, change himself, in order to be known by this place. And he, 'Efraim Nisan, close to three in the morning, was ready to exchange the whole of his legacy for one day, one hour of total inner freedom and feeling at home.'

In their Other World, as writers, Naguib Mahfouz, Chinua Achebe, and Amos Oz have the compulsion, the integrity and the audacity to answer the call of The Concealed Side, go too far, after Zaabalawi in pursuit of the truth, the Forgotten Promised Land where their peoples could appease an embittered history.

6

THAT OTHER WORLD THAT WAS THE WORLD

More than three hundred years of the colonization of modern times (as distinct from the colonization of antiquity) have come to an end. This is the positive achievement of our twentieth century, in which so much has been negative, so much suffering and destruction has taken place. Colonization is passing into history, except for comparatively small pockets of the earth's surface where new conquest has taken a precarious hold and the conquered, far from being subdued into acquiescence, make life for the conquerors difficult and dangerous.

Surely the grand finale of the age of colonization took place in the three years, 1991 to 1994, when South Africa emerged amazingly, a great spectacle of human liberation, from double colonization.

For unlike other countries where the British, the French, the Portuguese and other European powers ruled the indigenous people and when these colonizers were defeated or withdrew, left the countries in indigenous hands, South Africa in the early twentieth century passed from colonization from without—Dutch, French, finally British—to perpetuated colonization within, in the form of white minority power over the black majority. All the features of colonization were retained: taxes and the appropriation of land by whites, so that blacks would have to come to town and provide cheap labour in order to survive; favoured status for the minority in civil rights, education, freedom of movement. Freed from British imperialism, South Africa was far from free; it was a police state based on the claim that the white skin of colonials was superior to black skin.

I think there is a definite distinction to be made, everywhere, between what were the first settlers, the so-called pioneers who fought their way into a country, killing Indians or blacks, and the people of later generations who were born into a society that had long established its ruling accommodation with the indigenous people: a society removed from all danger, that had made itself comfortable with injustice, in this case the theory that there are genetically inferior races with lower needs than others.

I emerged into this milieu with my birth in South Africa in the Twenties. I shall never write an autobiography—I'm much too jealous of my privacy, for that—but I begin to think that my experience as a product of this social phenomenon has relevance beyond the personal; it may be a modest part of alternative history if pieced together with the experience of other writers. And it has a conclusion I did not anticipate would be reached in my lifetime, even when I became aware of my situation.

We lived in a small gold-mining town thirty miles from

Johannesburg, lost in the veld nearly 6,000 feet above sea level. The features of the landscape, its shapes and volumes, were made of waste. We were surrounded by yellow geometrical dumps of gold tailings and black hills of coal slag. I thought it ugly when I was a child brought up on English picture books of lush meadows and woods—but now I find the vast grassland beautiful and the memory of it an intimation to me, if I had known it then, that the horizons of existence are wide and that the eye and the mind could be carried on and on, from there.

My mother came from England when she was six years old. My father came from Latvia at thirteen. She had a solid, petty middle-class, piano-playing background, a father lured to emigration by the adventure of diamond prospecting rather than need. My father was sent away by his father to escape pogroms and poverty.

Perhaps because of their youth when they left, and because of this economic and social disparity, my parents kept no connections with the countries they emigrated from. They could not talk of a common 'home' across the water, as many other whites in the town did. My father was ashamed of his lack of formal education and my mother did not disguise the fact that she felt she had demeaned herself by marrying him. There was a certain dour tact in not talking about where they had sprung from.

Though both Jewish, they did not take part in Jewish communal life in the town, or join the Zionist associations of the time; they did not belong to a synagogue—my mother was an agnostic and my father, who had had an orthodox childhood, could not withstand her gibes about the hypocrisy of organized religion.

In one of Albert Camus's novels, the child Jacques, born and

116

living in Algeria, asks his mother: 'Maman, qu'est que c'est la patrie?' And she replies, 'Je ne sais pas. Non.' And the child says, 'C'est la France.'

If I had been asked the question as a child, I probably would have said, 'It's England.' South Africa's British dominion status had ended the year after I was born, but South Africa was a 'sovereign independent state' whose allegiance still was to the British Crown. At school we celebrated the Twenty-fifth Jubilee of 'our' King, George V. The so-called mother country: that was the focus of inculcated loyalty, of allegiance, identification for English-speaking South Africans.

And yet it was so remote, that England, that Northern Hemisphere we learnt about in geography class. In the Twenties and Thirties it was four weeks away across the seas. We were at the bottom of the map; we did not count, had little sense of ourselves beyond the performance of daily life.

Italo Calvino was not a colonial but he knew the sense an imaginative child, living in a small town even in an integrated, Italian society, may have of living in an ante-room of life. He describes how, as a boy, passing the cinema where dubbed voices on the sound track of American films came through the projectionist's window, he could 'sense the call of that other world that was the world.'

This conveys perfectly, at a graver and more enduring—a damaging level—what was my sense of my own existence.

From a very early age I had the sense that that other world—the world of books I took from the library, the world of the cinema—was that other world that was the world. We lived outside it.

It called. Perhaps some day, if one were very lucky, very good, worked very hard, one might get to see it; and as I grew older that world took form, Dickens's and Virginia Woolf's London, Balzac's and Proust's Paris. As for America, I passed from Huck Finn to Faulkner and Eudora Welty; but America was not on the itinerary of the retired mine captains and shift bosses and their wives, my mother's friends, who saved all their lives to afford one trip 'home' to England on retirement.

That other world that was the world.

For me, this was not merely a charming childish romanticism; I would not simply grow out of it, grow into my own world effortlessly, as Calvino would.

I had no lineal connection with the past around me, the dynasties of black people.

I had the most tenuous of connections with the present in which I was growing up.

My parents never talked politics; the only partisanship they displayed was during the war, when they wanted 'la patrie', the British, to defeat the Germans. I was not even dimly aware of the preparation for the struggle for political power that was beginning between Afrikaners, who more than twenty years before my birth had lost the Boer War to the British, and English-speaking South African whites who were the victors.

I saw the bare-foot children of poor-white Afrikaners, victims of defeat and drought, selling newspapers, just as I saw black people, victims of a much greater defeat, the theft of their land and the loss of all rights over the conduct of their lives, sent back to their ghetto after the day's work serving the town.

Reading a biography of Marguerite Duras recently, I see in her colonial childhood in Indochina my own in South Africa. Her family 'had the right not to be kept waiting at administration counters, and were served everywhere before the local Vietnamese. They benefited by the privileges reserved for the

French colonials. Marguerite does not complain about this difference in treatment. The distinction between the races is a natural reality for her.'

As it was for me.

What was my place? Could it know me?

On the one hand there was that other world that was the world, where Ginger Rogers and Fred Astaire danced in a cloudscape (I had ambitions to be a dancer, myself, as an entry to that world) and Maurice Chevalier sang about Paris. There were the moors where Heathcliff's Kathy wandered, and the London park where Mrs Dalloway took her walks.

On the other hand, just outside the gate of our suburban house with its red-polished stoep and two bow-windows, there was the great continuous to-and-fro of life, the voice of it languages I didn't understand but that were part of my earliest aural awakening; the spectacle of it defined by my adult mentors as something nothing to do with me.

This totally surrounding, engulfing experience was removed from me not by land and sea but by law, custom and prejudice.

And fear. I was told by my mother to avoid passing, on my way to school, the mine compound where black miners lived; she did not explain why, but the reason seeped to me through adult innuendo: there was the idea that every black man was waiting to rape some toothy little white schoolgirl.

Many years later, my friend and fellow writer Es'kia Mphahlele told me he was instructed by his mother to turn his bicycle down another street if he saw he was going to pass white boys. He did not know why until, in the same way as I learned my fear of black men, he gathered that he must believe every white was only waiting for the opportunity to attack him.

There was certainly more substance behind the fear instilled

❦

in him than the fear instilled in me, since blacks were physically maltreated by some whites; but the extreme unlikelihood that he or I was in any danger in the manner anticipated was part of the paranoia of separation that prevailed, matched each to the colour of his or her skin.

Archbishop Desmond Tutu—he and I have discovered—as a child lived for some time in the black ghetto across the veld from the town where I, too, was growing up; there was as much chance of our meeting then as there was of a moon landing.

Did we pass one another, sometimes, on Saturday mornings when the white town and the black ghetto all stocked up for the weekend at the same shops? Did I pass him by when I went into the local library to change books, a library he was barred from because he was black?

Perhaps there were explanations for all this, but they were not evident at home, at school, or among the contemporaries who were chosen for me, to whom I was confined by law, so to speak. And if there were to be some explanations in that other world that was the world, over the seas, it was not open to me; you could not expect it to be bothered with us.

Albert Camus's unfinished, posthumously published novel, from which I quoted earlier, has what appears to be a puzzling title, *Le Premier Homme;* but this is not some Neanderthal romance. Jacques is a colonial boy born and growing up in Algiers. He's white, not Arab; therefore, as we have seen in his answer to his mother, he must be French. But he has never seen France. For fictional Jacques and for the child I was, the premise is: Colonial: that's the story of who I am.

The one who belongs nowhere.

The one who has no national mould.

As Jacques grows up he comes to the realization that he must *make himself*. The precept is: if he is not to be the dangling participle of imperialism, if he is not to be the outsider defined by Arabs—a being non-Arab—what is he? A negative. In this sense, he starts from zero. He is the constructor of his own consciousness. He is The First Man.

Let us not worry about the gender: I was to come to the same necessity; to *make myself,* in the metaphor of The First Man, without coherent references, up on his own two legs, no model on how to proceed.

Of course the realization of the necessity did not come quickly; one must not exaggerate, or rather one cannot exaggerate sufficiently the tendency of human beings to keep sipping the daily syrup of life in a cosy enclave.

Our place as whites outside that world that was the world, overseas, was suitably humble—what effrontery to think that we could write a poem or compose a song that would be 'good enough', over there—but ours was a place secure and comfortable, so long as one kept to the simple rules, not walking by too close to the compound where the black miners lived. The ordinary components of childhood were mine, at least until the age of eleven when circumstances that have no relevance here put a curious end to it.

But with every adolescence there comes to everyone the inner tug of war—the need to break away, and the need to bond.

I had more passionate emotion for the first than courage to carry it out, but that would have resolved itself anyway, with time and confidence.

What was dismaying was the lack of discovery of what one might turn *to,* bond *with.*

121

Young white people in the town gathered in sports clubs and religious groups; they met the same people at tennis on Sunday as they had danced with on Saturday night. It was a prelude to going to one another's weddings, attending bridge afternoons and charity cake-sales (the white women) and meeting to exchange chaff in the club bar after golf (the white men). As Camus says, a life 'with no other project but the immediate.'

A life ordered, defined, circumscribed by the possession of a white skin. I did not know anything else, yet I knew I could not commit myself there; I felt it as a vague but menacing risk, bondage, not bonding. My reaction was to retreat, turn even further away from the reality of our life than the club life of colonials, which at least was an enclave within the life that swarmed around it.

That world that was the world, overseas, now lived my life as proxy for me; it was no longer the cloudscape of Fred Astaire and Ginger Rogers, but the world of literature. I ate and slept at home, but I had my essential being in books. Rilke roused and answered the emptiness in me where religious faith was missing. Chekhov and Dostoevsky opened for me the awesome mysteries of human behaviour. Proust taught me that sexual love, for which every adolescent yearns, is a painful and cruel affair as well as the temptation of bliss. Yeats made me understand there was such a thing as a passion for justice, quite as strong as sexual passion.

These and other writers were my mentors, out of whom I tried to make an artificial construct of myself. When young people are said to 'live in books' rather than in themselves, this is regarded as an escape; it is more likely a search.

For me, of course, the search was not a success in terms of the unconscious purpose I had. I could not make myself out of the components of that other world, though I could and did appropriate it for my delight and enlightenment. What it could do for me, and did, was turn me to face a possibility; a possibility for myself. In my desire to write, in the writing that I was already doing out of my pathetically limited knowledge of the people and the country where I lived, was the means to find what my truth was, what was there to bond with, how I could manage to become my own First Man, woman-man, human being.

I had, in fact, been engaged with this possibility for some time, without understanding what I was doing.

An early story of mine harked back to a childhood impression I had thought forgotten.

On that same way to school when I avoided crossing the path of the black miners in the open veld, I would pass the row of 'Concession' stores—trading concessions on mine property—which served the miners and had the intended effect of keeping them out of the town. I had taken my time, as children will dawdle, seeing through the shop doors every day how the miners were treated by the white shopkeepers, spoken to abusively, not allowed to linger in choice of purchases as we whites did. At the time, to me this was just another example of the way adult life was ordered; something accepted, not disturbing. But the images had fermented below the surface impressions of childhood as I developed the writer's questioning concentration.

What I was coming to understand, in writing that story, was one of the essential features of colonialism: the usefulness to the regime of the poor immigrant's opportunity, at last, to feel superior to someone, and thereby support the regime's policy of keeping the indigenous population decreed inferior.

ᴎ

My story's title was 'The Defeated'; and it did not refer only to the black miners. They were despised, and bullied across the counter by white immigrants who themselves had a precarious economic and social footing: ill-educated, scarcely able to speak the two languages of the white community, carrying in their minds and bodies the humiliations and deprivation of pogroms and quotas they had fled in Eastern Europe.

In keeping with my ignorance at the time, the story makes too much of an equation between the defeated—the shop-keeper who relieves his feelings of inferiority within the white community by maltreating blacks, the black miners who are so stripped of every context of human dignity that they must submit to abuse even from someone at the lowest level in the white community.

For the shopkeeper and the black miner were, in fact, *not* in the same social pit.

I could have written a sequel set ten or twenty years on and the shopkeeper would have had a business in town and a son at a university, he would have been a naturalized full citizen with the vote—while the black miner still would have been drilling the rock-face or back in his rural home living on the meagre savings of a lifetime spent underground, and still with-out citizenship rights or the vote in the country of his birth and ancestry.

But if out of a muddled desire to juggle justice where there was none—a kind of reconciliatory conclusion I might have thought was the correct literary approach—I equated the meas-ure of defeat in the lives of the two men, black and white, I did at least reveal in the story that important phenomenon whereby the balance of oppression is maintained not just by laws, but in every situation of social intercourse. I was learning that oppression thrives on all manner of prejudicial behaviour, is fostered by all kinds of insecurity.

With small beginnings such as this I started, tentatively, held back by the strictly controlled environment of the white enclave, to live in the country to which, until then, I had no claim but the fact of birth.

In my stories I was continuing to turn over, this way and that, events in the conduct of my narrow life that had seemed to have a single meaning. The only communal activity in which I'd taken part was amateur theatricals; the first uneasy stirrings of liberalism in the town came to be expressed in the mode the churches and individual consciences were accustomed to—charity. No one thought to petition the town council to open the library to blacks, but it was decided to take a play to the only public hall in the black ghetto.

The play was *The Importance of Being Earnest,* and I had the role of Gwendolen. I was twenty and had never been into a black township before; I believe none of us in the cast had. I believe that no one in the audience had ever seen a play before; how could they? The Town Hall, which doubled as a theatre, was closed to blacks. The audience started off close-kneed and hands folded but was soon laughing and exclaiming. We thought we had had a great success, and drank to it back-stage with our usual tipple, some gaudy liqueur.

When the scenes of that evening kept returning to me in aspects turned this way and that, and I began to write a piece of fiction, make a story out of them, what emerged was a satire—on us.

On the absurdity of taking what we imagined was bountiful cultural uplift, an Oscar Wilde play, to the ghetto the town had created. I came to the full appreciation that the audience, those

125

people with drama, tragedy and comedy in their own lives about which we knew *nothing,* were laughing at us.

Not at the play, but us. They did not understand the play with its elaborate, facetious and ironic use of the language they half-knew, English; but they understood *us,* all right. And we in our pretensions, our idea of what we were 'giving' them, were exquisitely funny. Oscar Wilde perhaps would have been amused to think that his play became doubly a satire, functioning as such far from Lady Bracknell's drawing-room.

I think I have been fortunate in that I was born into the decadence of the colonial period.

It has been ravelling out during my lifetime. This is so, even though the mid-century saw the hardening of South African racism in huge forced removals of the black population in order to satisfy white separatism and economic greed, the outlawing of all opposition to these policies as subversion, and for millions the suffering of imprisonment and exile. These were the ghastly paroxysms of a monstrous regime thrashing about in death throes.

The reaction of the white community to strikes and mass demonstrations was to raise the drawbridges over which blacks might commingle with whites. Sexual relations between black and white became a criminal offence, no mixed membership of political parties was allowed, even ambulances were segregated so that an accident victim might lie by the roadside until the vehicle mandated to the appropriate skin colour could be summoned.

A larger and larger army and police force were deployed to keep blacks out of white lives, and all the devices of bugging, opening mail, infiltrating, trapping, spying were gratefully tolerated by the white community within itself for what it believed was its own safety. For, of course, there were dissidents among whites who actively supported blacks against discrimination, and who, going about undetected in their white skin, could be hunted out only in this way.

But no piling-up of restrictive laws, no recruitment of professional liars, stool-pigeons and psychopath interrogators, no population removals could stop the historical process of unravelling. The population removals brought more and more people illegally into the cities, since they could not subsist in the barren areas they were banished to. Arrested, sent away, they came back again. No console of listening and watching devices discouraged dissidents in the white community; merely sharpened their skills at, in turn, evading detection of their communications and contacts, at home, with the banned black liberation movement, and with its supporters abroad. No bans on the mixing of black and white could stop the reaction to the ultimate in inhuman segregation that we were living: there was the violent urge to separation, and the counter urge it set up: the urge to move towards blacks, not alone as a matter of justice, but as a human imperative.

When I had longed to get out of the small town which did not know me, my perceptions of it setting me apart, I had envisaged this as a move that would bring me closer to that other world that was the world—European ideas, mores. Johannesburg, the city, was surely at least the local representative of that world. But by the time I made the move to Johannesburg it was to bring me closer not to Europe, but to the discovery of what could be my own country; closer to the appropriation that was all that I rightfully could begin to lay claim to. As whites, we had moved away officially from the claim of a 'mother country' across the seas—we were even to leave the British Commonwealth in the 1960s. I could now speak of 'my country', and mean South Africa.

But it was not possible for me to say 'my people.' That I began to understand.

The whites were not my people because everything they lived by—their claimed racial superiority and the methods they were satisfied to use to maintain it as if it were truth—was the stuff of my refusal. And they did not recognize refusal as a valid position. Refusal was treason.

The blacks were not 'my people' because all through my childhood and adolescence they had scarcely entered my consciousness. *I had been absent.* Absent from them.

Could one, in fact, make the claim, 'my country' if one could not also say 'my people'?

The breaches and interstices that the ravelling-out of apartheid colonialism produced, even while it fanatically shored itself up, were being rapidly invaded. The African National Congress, which since its founding in 1912 had gone through the revolutionary evolution from a self-help ethic to mass passive resistance campaigns, and finally the 1961 decision to take up armed struggle, went Underground when it was banned. From there it tunnelled beneath successive white governments. So did the other banned liberation movements, the Pan Africanist Congress, and the South African Communist Party, which was also part of the command of the African National Congress's military wing, Umkhonto we Sizwe, 'Spear of the Nation.'

While this political revolution was taking place despite—indeed, because of the treason trials, bannings and banishments with which the State tried literally to shoot it down—there were other, insidious, invasions penetrating the security system into which whites had withdrawn their bodies and minds.

In the Fifties when I came to live in Johannesburg, one of the points of entry was Bohemianism. A quaint, outdated import from the Europe of several generations back, yes, but serving a different purpose, in South Africa's largest city.

We were not starving artists living in garrets and defying the bourgeois values of some integrated society. We were young people starved of contact with one another by innumerable barriers of law and custom and fear. We did not know how to go about putting our country, ourselves, together—that was the half-understood motive. We broke the easiest taboos first. Black musicians, teachers, journalists, aspirant writers met their white counterparts to talk, drink and dance—the two latter rituals standard as the preparation for many different kinds of human intercourse. We gathered in old factory premises clandestinely decked out as clubs; in whites' houses, where blacks were forbidden to be except as servants; and in the black shebeens hidden in the city.

The blacks came from the ghettoes of Soweto and Alexandra and from the streets of the old mining camp quarters of the city where people of all colours once had lived, and which were being bulldozed to establish white occupation only. The whites were young men and women like myself. The mild risks we took, of discovery and prosecution, were our adventure: a prelude to commitment to revolution.

Of course, there were white people who were dedicated revolutionaries in the South African Communist Party and other, minor, Left groupings, and who became the hunted when all liberation movements were outlawed. The Communist Party had members of all colours; the African National

Congress did not openly have white membership, but a devoted group of whites, growing over the years, worked within it.

I did not join or commit myself formally to a liberation movement in that period, no doubt out of fear—a new fear in a way of life new to me, then; still there was the lingering colonial conditioning that revolution was the blacks' affair. But at the same time, in mixing more and more with blacks, sharing with them as aspirant writers, painters and actors the sense of *learning how to think* outside the way our society was ordered, I was going through a personal revolution that had no other issue but to lead me into theirs; to find myself, there.

Where there is the necessity, through historical circumstance of time, place and birth, to 'make oneself' many processes take place at once. Because I had turned out to be a writer, because I was just that, because it was my fundament beneath all that had been done to condition my being, all my confusions, my false consciousness—because I was a writer, my principal means of 'making myself' was my writing.

Only through the writer's explorations could I have begun to discover the human dynamism of the place I was born to and the time in which it was to be enacted. Only in the prescient dimension of the imagination could I bring together what had been deliberately broken and fragmented; fit together the shapes of living experience, my own and that of others, without which a whole consciousness is not attainable. I had to be part of the *transformation of my place* in order for it to know me.

This does not mean that I saw my way as a crusader, writing to expose injustice, a polemicist and propagandist. My compre-

130

hension of life had been kept so narrow, everything in it painted white—white morality, white customs, white habits, white values; once free of that, I had the writer's healthy selfish instinct to keep open the multiple vision that the fly's eye of the writer had brought me.

There were so many human drives and emotions that had been unknown to me, because life sheltered in the white enclave did not have, or did not see the necessity to take on, the situations which brought these forth. What did I know about courage? It was something associated with illness—'borne courageously'—or war; in the small town I had left behind me there were men with medals. But in the life of clandestine involvement with black men and women, one found that courage was a daily commodity.

A black had to have courage to risk arrest for being in the streets after curfew or leaving a town to find work in another; the courage to get up at three in the morning every day to travel from some distant ghetto to work in the city; the courage to go back to school after spending years at menial labour so that a brother or sister might have a spell of education; the courage to live without privacy, to create self-respect without personal space, the terrible ordeal of slum living.

And out of this taken-for-granted courage came a capacity to live life through to the full that I had not known among whites. This vitality, informing my writing because I was now open to it, affirmed in fiction—the truth that is in fiction—the reality that was rising beneath the repression. The expression in art of *what really exists* beneath the surface is part of the transformation of a society. What is written, painted, sung, cannot remain ignored.

131

❦

And where was that other world that was the world, during that period? Came the day when that other world that was the world sought *us* out.

Of course, they had been here before: 'discovered' natural features and places by giving European names to what already had been named by people who had lived here since antiquity. Those of us who were white were even descended from these explorers: we'd never have been here if they had not opened a way. But this time when they came it was not to plant flags or name, neither was it to see Table Mountain and the wild-life parks.

It was to tour *us*. Our lives were the artifacts they took home: to recount, to display in discourse, as previous tourists would have hung masks and bead-work. Just as there is now ecological tourism, there was in the Sixties, Seventies and Eighties revolutionary tourism. Come and see the banned, the restricted, in their own habitat.

❦

Without my making any display of political commitment, my writing became the 'essential gesture' of the writer to her or his society of which Roland Barthes speaks. It was with my stories and novels, my offering of what I was learning about the life within me and around me, that I entered the commonality of my country.

As a consequence, some of my books were banned. Of course, that was not enough; I was a citizen as well as a writer, I was white and living in the privilege decreed by my skin. If I were to 'live to the full' this contradiction of my time it was necessary for me to act, as well, in forms other than writing.

Personal friendships that ignored the taboos of colour were

only the beginning of taking responsibility for what was being done in the name of white skin; what was implied was the obligation to oppose and destroy the power of racism in its seat of government. The party was over—the happy defiance in drinking and dancing; there came the need to hide people from the police, to help people flee over the border—both treasonable offences—to forget the old white middle-class guilt about lying—what was their petty standard of truth when the entire platform of their life was the lie of superiority?

There was the need to forget that so-called morality and learn to live deviously for the survival of others, and oneself.

For years I did these things, always conscious that what I did was not enough. I became a small component in the vast movement where millions, shunted about the country, imprisoned, banned, cast into exile, tear-gassed and shot, yet trudged towards the end of colonialism in its final avatar, South African racism.

And still I was aware that although I could say 'my country'—blacks did not dispute the claim of birthright—I could not say 'my people.'

Until every law that set me aside from black people was abolished, until we were all to be born and pursue our lives everywhere in the same right, governed by the free choice of all the people, my place would not know me. No matter how I and others like me conducted ourselves, we were held in the categories of the past. The laws that provided that more money be spent on a white child's education than on a black's, that a white worker be paid more than a black worker, that black people could be transported like livestock to exist where whites decreed—all this had to go.

The exiles had to come back to their rightful home; the

prisoners of conscience had to be received on the mainland from Robben Island, and to walk out of Pollsmoor prison; those who had been harried and cast out had to take up the seats of power where their persecutors had ruled so long.

It came to pass.

It is not only in a religious sense that one may be born again. In 1994 the struggle, the final process of decolonization was achieved, after decades when the end receded again and again. In April 1994 all South Africans of all colours went to the polls and voted into power their own government, for the first time. There are now no overlords and underlings in the eyes of the law. What this means to our millions is something beyond price or reckoning that we know we shall have to work to put into practice, just as we worked for liberation. We know we have to perform what Flaubert called 'the most difficult and least glamorous of all tasks: transition.' This is the reality of freedom. This is the great matter.

I am a small matter; but for myself there is something immediate, extraordinary, of strong personal meaning. That other world that was the world is no longer the world. My country is the world, whole, a synthesis. I am no longer a colonial. I may now speak of 'my people.'

Notes

Index

NOTES

1. Adam's Rib

Page

5   *a metaphysical mirror:* Primo Levi, *The Mirror Maker: Stories & Essays,* trans. Raymond Rosenthal (New York: Schocken Books, 1989), p. 51.

6   *a book is not about:* Henrik Ibsen; from my notebooks; source not identified.

6   *When I came to write:* Graham Greene; from my notebooks; source not identified. Probably *A Sort of Life* (London: Bodley Head, 1971).

6   *rescue work:* Joseph Conrad, in an essay on Henry James, quoted in Edward W. Said, *Joseph Conrad and the Fiction of Autobiography* (Cambridge, Mass.: Harvard University Press, 1966), p. 10. *What is a novel:* ibid., p. 123.

8   *inventory of elements . . . bundle of transformations:* Jean Piaget, 'Structural Analysis and the Social Studies', in *Structuralism,* trans. Chaminah Maschler (London: Routledge & Kegan Paul, 1968), p. 119.

12   *duality of inwardness:* Georg Lukács, *The Theory of the Novel* (London: Merlin Press, 1971).

12   *there is a limit:* Quoted in Jordan Elgrably, 'Conversations with Milan Kundera', *Salmagundi,* no. 73 (Winter 1987), p. 24.

13   *a discrete analogy . . . To put forth:* Said, *Joseph Conrad and the Fiction of Autobiography; In this manner:* ibid.

〰

14 *The ability of writers:* Toni Morrison, *Playing in the Dark: Whiteness and the Literary Imagination* (Cambridge, Mass.: Harvard University Press, 1992), p. 15.

14 *is the only method:* Georg Lukács, *History and Class Consciousness* (London: Merlin Press, 1971), p. 10.

14 *writing and life:* Said, *Joseph Conrad and the Fiction of Autobiography.*

15 *What is told:* Roland Barthes, *S/Z* (London: Jonathan Cape, 1975), p. 213.

15 *Culture and Imperialism:* Edward W. Said, *Culture and Imperialism* (New York: Knopf, 1993).

16 *to interpret:* Barthes, *S/Z,* p. 5; *semantic space:* ibid., p. 61; *producer of the text:* ibid., p. 4.

17 *lexia:* Roland Barthes defines lexia as 'a series of brief, contiguous fragments' (ibid., p. 13). The word is the translator's version of the French term, *lexie.*

18 *A metonymy leads:* ibid., p. 21.

18 *Words are symbols:* Jorge Luis Borges, 'The Congress', in *The Book of Sand,* trans. Norman Thomas di Giovanni (Harmondsworth: Penguin, 1982), p. 33.

19 *to use fiction:* Frank Kermode, Preface to Robert Musil's *Five Women* (Boston: David R. Godine, Nonpareil Books, 1986).

2. Hanging on a Sunrise

20 *Are we approaching:* Nadine Gordimer, *The Black Interpreters* (Johannesburg: Spro-Cas/Ravan, 1973), p. 7.

23 *The struggle of man:* Milan Kundera, *The Book of Laughter and Forgetting,* trans. Michael Henry Heim (Harmondsworth: Penguin, 1981).

24 *To write:* Henrik Ibsen; from my notebooks; source not identified.

25 *Terror is the outgrowth:* Georg Büchner, *Complete Plays and Prose* (New York: Hill & Wang, 1963).

26 *watched from the shadows:* Ronnie Kasrils, *'Armed and Dangerous': My Underground Struggle against Apartheid* (London: Heinemann, 1993), p. 3.

29 *The question:* ibid., p. 253.

31 *'They' are members:* Carl Niehaus, *Fighting for Hope,* trans. Ethne Clark (Cape Town and Johannesburg: Human and Rousseau, 1993), p. 8; *In times:* ibid., p. 18.

32 *The danger of losing:* ibid., p. 19; *My own excitement . . . the filthy compound . . . whenever I managed . . . Amidst the sounds:* ibid., pp. 40–41.

33 *was convinced:* ibid., p. 94; *I was worried:* ibid., pp. 106–107.

౹౹

34 *because we had not:* ibid., p. 112; *Suddenly:* ibid., p. 136.

35 *We make of the quarrel:* W. B. Yeats; from my notebooks; source not identified.

36 *I think:* Jeremy Cronin, untitled, in *Inside* (Johannesburg: Ravan Press, 1983), p. 23; *There we are:* 'Group Photo from Pretoria Local on the Occasion of a Fourth Anniversary (Never Taken)', ibid., pp. 21–22.

37 *you commune:* 'For Comrades in Solitary Confinement', ibid., p. 25; *this thing:* 'In the Naval Base', ibid., p. 39; *I check:* 'Poem-Shrike', ibid., p. 3.

38 *There is no way:* Mongane Wally Serote, *A Tough Tale* (London: Kliptown Books, 1987), p. 31.

39 *We/We are men:* ibid., p. 22.

39 *so-and-so is pissing:* Mongane Wally Serote, *Third World Express* (Cape Town: David Philip Publishers, 1992), p. 27.

39 *We want the world:* Serote, *A Tough Tale,* p. 7.

39 *In the heart:* Serote, *Third World Express,* p. 1.

40 *despair:* ibid., p. 25; *blacks and whites:* ibid., pp. 27–28.

41 *What can we do:* ibid., pp. 20–21.

42 *metahistory:* Octavio Paz, 'Imperial Democracy', in *One Earth, Four or Five Worlds: Reflections on Contemporary History* (New York: Harcourt Brace Jovanovich, 1992), p. 30.

42 *One morning:* Serote, *A Tough Tale,* pp. 43–44.

3. Zaabalawi: The Concealed Side

43 *Do not be afraid:* Marcel Proust; from my notebooks; source not identified.

44 *God be with you:* Naguib Mahfouz, 'Zaabalawi', in *Time and the Place and Other Stories,* trans. Denys Johnson-Davies (Garden City, N.Y.: Doubleday, 1991), p. 7. *Yes I have to find:* ibid., p. 14.

45 *his place:* Amos Oz, *Fima* (London: Chatto & Windus, 1993), p. 123. *sitra de-itkasia:* ibid., p. 207.

46 *Cairo Trilogy:* Naguib Mahfouz, *Palace Walk, Palace of Desire, Sugar Street: The Cairo Trilogy* (Garden City, N.Y.: Doubleday/Anchor, 1991, 1991, 1993).

46 *with the same enthusiasm:* Mahfouz, *Palace Walk,* p. 17.

47 *he strove to keep:* ibid., p. 130; *Gentlemen:* ibid., p. 268; *Despite his number:* ibid., p. 99.

48 *Thirst for love:* ibid., p. 85.

48 *the only interview:* at the time of writing; after the attack on his life Mahfouz gave several interviews.

〜

48   *What is the subject:* Charlotte El Shabrawy, 'The Art of Fiction: Naguib Mahfouz', interview, *Paris Review,* no. 123 (Summer 1992).

49   *Why don't you:* Mahfouz, *Palace Walk,* p. 161.

50   *May God destroy:* ibid., p. 39; *But what will you say:* ibid., p. 56.

51   *I'm so happy:* ibid., p. 330; *He could not have stood:* ibid., p. 357; *a friend:* ibid., pp. 421–422; *break every link:* ibid., p. 425.

52   *Don't mistake me:* ibid., p. 425.

53   *returned to his original:* Mahfouz, *Palace of Desire,* p. 82.

54   *Desire:* ibid.; *each massively beautiful:* ibid., p. 78; *I instinctively hate:* ibid., p. 41; *These people:* ibid., p. 39.

55   *It is marriage:* ibid., p. 19.

56   *A nation:* ibid., p. 178; *Strangely enough:* ibid., p. 227.

57   *You're not a prisoner:* ibid., p. 163; *Where's religion . . . Couldn't you find . . . Why had he written:* ibid., p. 336; *What was left:* ibid., p. 343.

58   *The Believer:* ibid., p. 344; *Is there anything:* ibid., p. 347; *A discharge:* ibid., pp. 352–353.

59   *Happiness:* ibid., p. 354; *The problem's:* ibid., p. 358.

59   *Althusser recounts:* Louis Althusser, *The Future Lasts Forever* (New York: The New Press, 1993).

59   *Man's a filthy creature:* Mahfouz, *Palace of Desire,* p. 367; *Man's a filthy creature?* ibid., p. 368.

60   *nothing but a drop:* ibid., p. 386; *Father:* ibid., pp. 372–375.

61   *In the distance:* ibid., p. 387; *for an effort . . . nothing more:* ibid., p. 388.

61   *sad to watch:* Mahfouz, *Sugar Street,* p. 9.

62   *in satisfying:* ibid., pp. 9–11; *His heart:* ibid., p. 29.

63   *We attempt:* ibid., p. 119; *Let us prepare:* ibid., p. 276; *Is talk:* ibid., p. 119; *Do you stone:* ibid., p. 120.

65   *as an unmarried teacher:* ibid., p. 185; *See how:* ibid., pp. 236–237; *How could . . . She was not:* ibid., pp. 256–257.

66   *he and his favourite:* ibid., p. 196; *Inside him:* ibid., p. 177.

67   *Am I cast . . . What could my offense . . . Here they were:* ibid., p. 301.

68   *Mysticism:* ibid., pp. 305–306; *Which way:* ibid., p. 307; *Art is the interpreter:* ibid., p. 138.

4. To Hold the Yam and the Knife

72   *How does the poor man . . . The very words:* Chinua Achebe, *Anthills of the Savannah* (Garden City, N.Y.: Doubleday/Anchor, 1988), p. 37; *undeserved accoutrements:* ibid., pp. 127–128.

❦

73 *sharply and decisively . . . I no tell you:* ibid., p. 128.

74 *alienated history:* ibid., p. 204; *The one in the front:* ibid., p. 60.

75 *glimpse a little light:* ibid., p. 42; *for reasons of his own:* ibid., p. 110.

76 *a game:* ibid., p. 2; *shifting-eyes people:* ibid., pp. 116–117.

77 *Once upon a time:* ibid., pp. 117–118.

78 *The sounding of the battle-drum:* ibid., pp. 113–114; *Resignation:* ibid., p. 133.

79 *I shall be born . . . a new explosion:* ibid., pp. 38–39.

80 *Lord Thy Word:* ibid., p. 39; *a political meditation . . . No doubt:* ibid., p. 141.

81 *whatever you are:* ibid., p. 142; *clear-eyed enough:* ibid., p. 146; *My view:* ibid., p. 149.

82 *overwhelming issue . . . how to counter . . . his place:* ibid., p. 156; *necessity:* ibid., p. 130; *one thousand:* ibid., p. 43; *To succeed:* ibid., p. 179; *A road accident:* ibid., p. 196.

84 *The women are:* ibid., p. 90.

85 *Experience and intelligence . . . None of this:* ibid., pp. 90–91.

87 *The choice:* Naguib Mahfouz, *Sugar Street* (Garden City, N.Y.: Doubleday/Anchor, 1993), p. 306.

88 *the traditions:* Achebe, *Anthills of the Savannah,* p. 96; *that we are surrounded . . . the moral nature:* ibid., p. 93; *the mystery of metaphor:* ibid., p. 94.

89 *But knowing . . . perhaps Ikem alone:* ibid., p. 96.

89 *known by one's place:* see Chapter 5, especially page 111.

91 *She picked up:* Achebe, *Anthills of the Savannah,* pp. 206–207.

92 *anthills of the savannah:* ibid., p. 28.

93 *we all imagine:* ibid., p. 114; *In his [the writer's] new-found utterance:* ibid., p. 115; *The explanation:* ibid., p. 204.

5. Forgotten Promised Land

94 *There is a forgotten promised land:* Amos Oz, *Fima* (London: Chatto & Windus, 1993), p. 78.

94 *What must a people do:* Chinua Achebe, *Anthills of the Savannah* (Garden City, N.Y.: Doubleday/Anchor, 1988), p. 204.

95 *less falsehood:* Oz, *Fima,* p. 1; *that the country:* ibid., p. 8.

96 *petty lies:* ibid., p. 1; *On the midday news . . . Although, in fact:* ibid., p. 12.

97 *the instant . . . Just stop:* ibid., pp. 12–13.

99 *transform Calcutta:* ibid., p. 54.

100 *What was the story . . . between revulsion:* ibid., pp. 30–31.

❧

101 *He visualized himself:* ibid., p. 8; *At the door:* ibid., p. 27.
102 *he stunned them . . . And from now on:* ibid., pp. 74–75.
103 *He saw no contradiction:* ibid., p. 61; *could almost hear:* ibid., p. 62.
104 *I asked . . . 'I'm not':* ibid., p. 66; *wounded roar . . . Baruch, you are blind:* ibid., p. 67.
105 *So what's wrong:* ibid., p. 67; *We've arranged:* ibid., p. 83; *In the middle:* ibid., pp. 85–86; *Automatic living:* ibid., pp. 100–101; *If he were Prime Minister:* ibid., p. 195.
106 *And how about you:* ibid., p. 101; *Everywhere we go:* ibid., p. 186.
107 *Suddenly a cockroach:* ibid., p. 71.
108 *Hey are you looking:* ibid., p. 207; *Once upon a time:* ibid., p. 216.
109 *The crime:* ibid., p. 220; *ultimate wakefulness . . that it might be:* ibid., p. 227.
110 *Don't be afraid:* ibid., p. 3; *He could see him:* ibid., p. 73.
111 *No more filthy kitchens:* ibid., p. 73; *his place:* ibid., p. 285.
112 *To grasp . . . the creator . . . aged about sixty:* ibid., p. 77.
113 *all those exciting objects . . . Efraim Nisan:* ibid., p. 297.

6. That Other World That Was the World

117 *Maman:* Albert Camus, *Le Premier Homme* (Paris: Gallimard, 1994), p. 191.
117 *sense the call:* Italo Calvino, 'A Cinema-goer's Autobiography', in *The Road to San Giovanni,* trans. Tim Parks (London: Jonathan Cape, 1993), p. 44.
118 *had the right:* 'les Donnadieu ont leurs passedroits. Ils n'attendent pas aux guichets des administrations, et sont servis partout en priorité sur les Annamites. Ils bénéficient des privilèges réservés, par principe, aux colons français. Marguerite ne se plaint pas de cette différence de traitement. La distinction des races est une réalité naturelle pour elle'; Frédérique Lebelley, *Marguerite Duras ou le Poids d'une Plume* (Paris: Grasset, 1994), p. 22.
122 *with no other project:* 'sans autre projet que l'immédiat'; Camus, *Le Premier Homme,* p. 182.
132 *essential gesture:* Roland Barthes, 'Writing Degree Zero', in *Barthes: Selected Writings* (London: Fontana, 1983), p. 31.
134 *the most difficult:* Gustave Flaubert; from my notebooks; source not identified; probably *The Letters of Gustave Flaubert*, 2 vols., trans. and ed. Francis Steegmuller (Cambridge, Mass.: The Belknap Press of Harvard University Press, 1980, 1982).

INDEX

143